The Digital Pilgrim

Matthew Adler

Matthew Adler
2012

E
BOOKS

Hardcover First Edition
ISBN 978-0-9831455-1-6

Published by Eagleburger Books
Durham, North Carolina
http://eagleburger.net

Cover Image: U.S. Defense Mapping Agency Topographic Center.

Contents

"The heavens declare the glory of God;
the skies proclaim the work of His hands.

Day after day they pour forth speech;
night after night they display knowledge.

There is no speech or language
where their voice is not heard.

Their voice goes out into all the earth,
their words to the ends of the world..."

– Psalm 19:1-4 (NIV)

Introduction

Not everyone believes that God is real. This is easy for me to understand. I have never seen God. I have never heard His voice. I am a scientist. It's hard to believe in things that can't be seen.

Yet, the world doesn't make sense without God. Randomness is an inadequate explanation for the demanding, particular conditions of our physical existence. The gospel message is taught by documents of exceeding historical veracity that contain prophecies unexplainable except by divine cause.

I can make many good arguments that God is real. I have expended immeasurable mental energy familiarizing myself with apologetics and trying to prove the case that God is there, but too often I treat God only as an academic subject. Too often I do not view Him as a person to be related to. Too often He is a tool to build my own understanding of the universe, not a Lord to rule me.

In contrast, the Bible, God's tool to speak directly to all of humanity, is filled with very little philosophy. It tells stories mostly, of real people in real places. If the Bible is a true book, then Jesus was a man. He was made of carbon and breathed oxygen. He lived and worked in places we can still identify today. He was very much a part of this mundane world that seemingly offers so little evidence of His existence.

God Himself does not describe our relationship in academic terms. Jesus did not come to answer our questions. He came to love us and to save us. Fortunately, our lives do not depend on our ability to reach a higher level of understanding. Our fate was decided by the historical actions of a real man. I want this book to illustrate His story.

The Desert, Sinai Peninsula

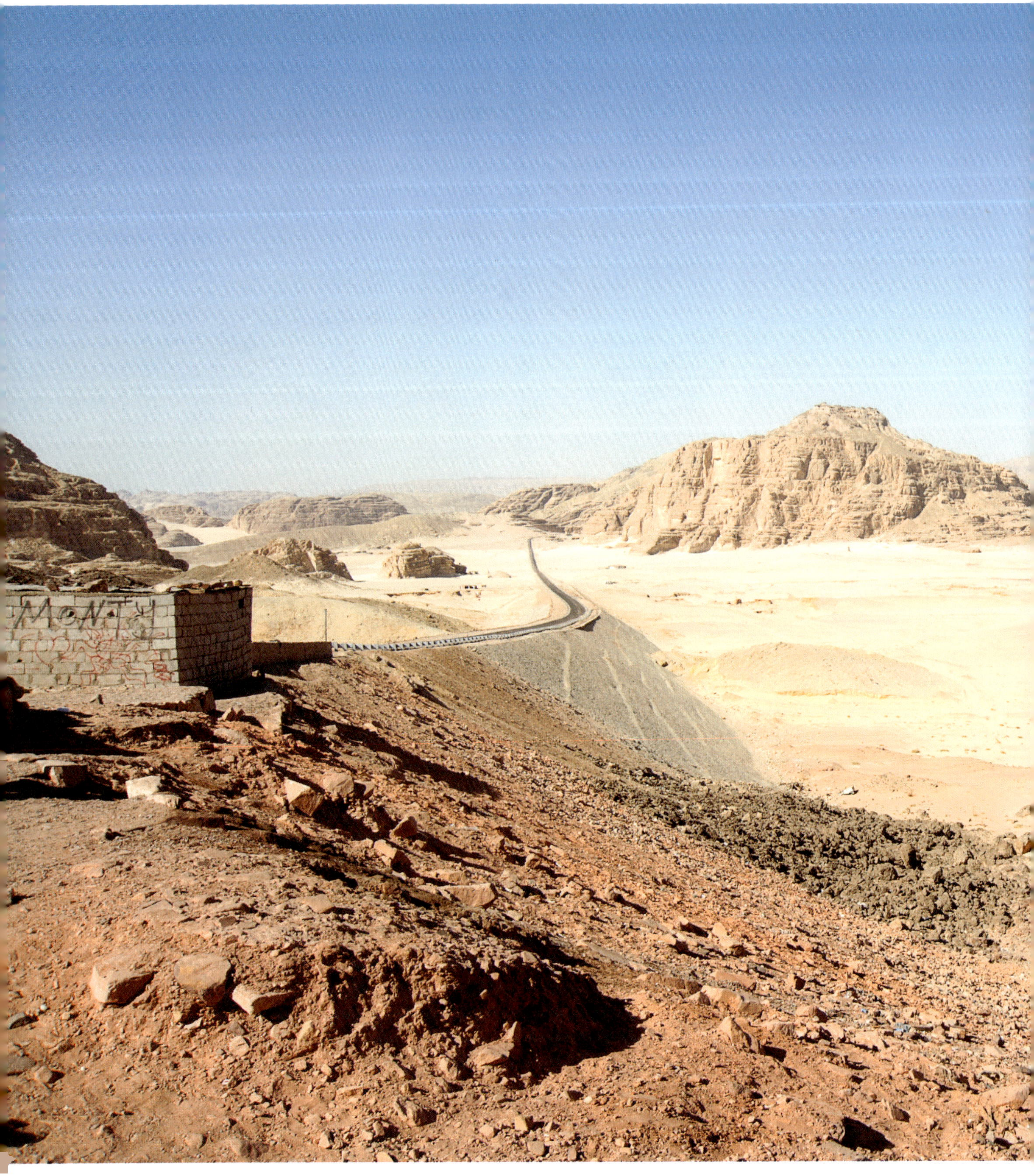

Egypt

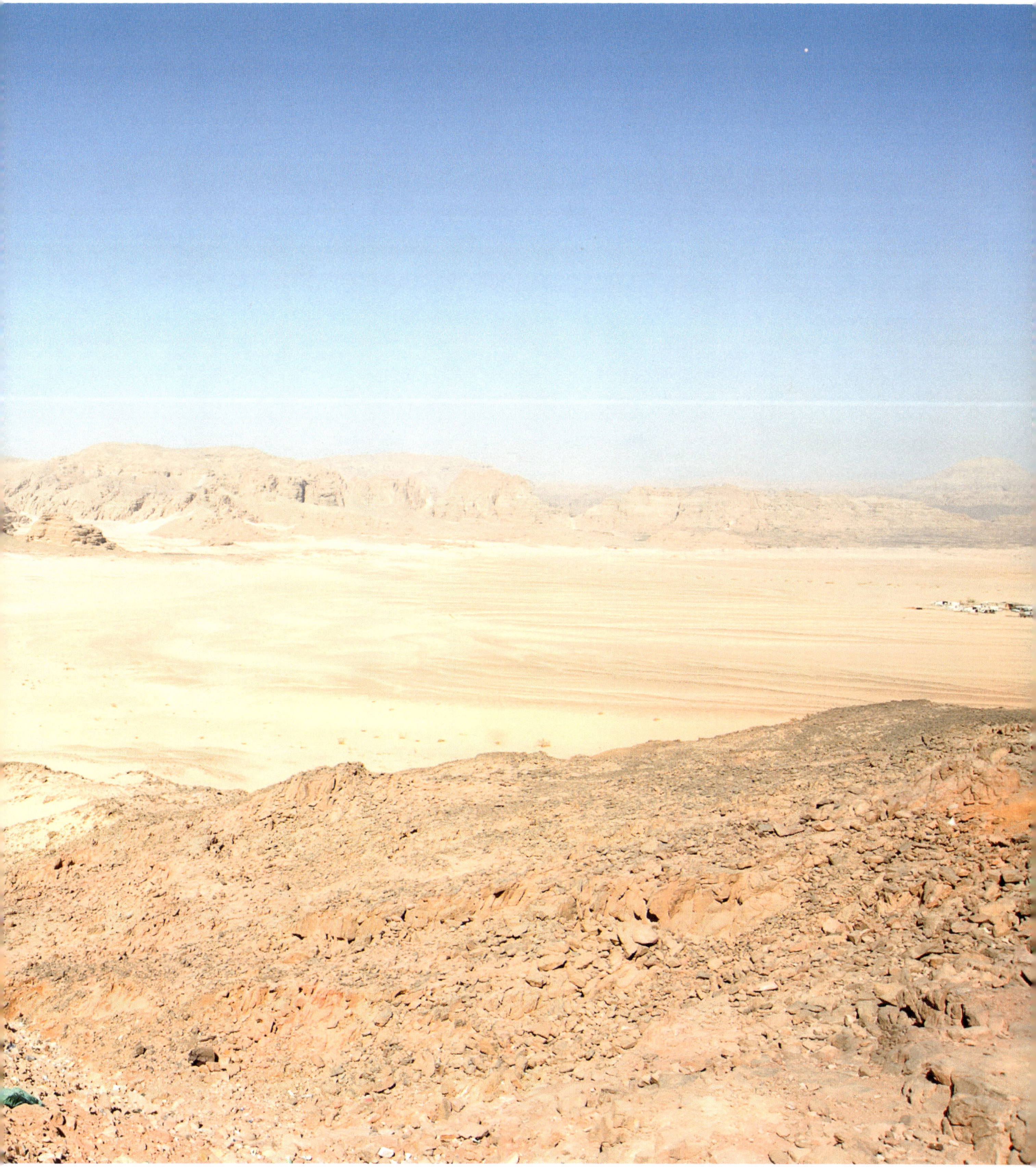

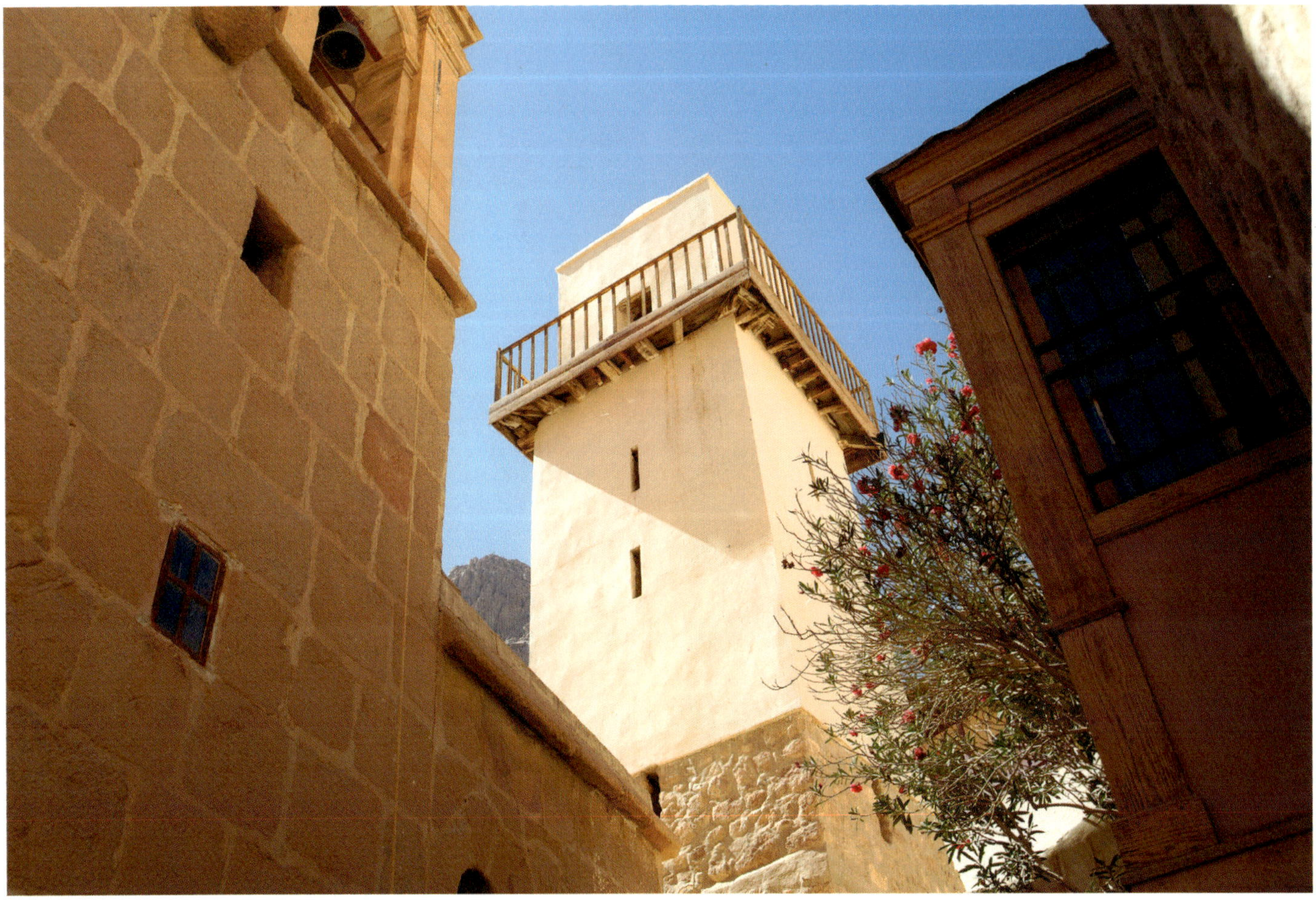

Pages 8-10: **St. Catherine's Monastery, Sinai Peninsula, Egypt**
This Orthodox monastery was built in the 6th century and is one of the world's oldest. It was constructed around the traditional location of Moses's burning bush and is on the foot of one of the mountains that may be the biblical Mt. Sinai.

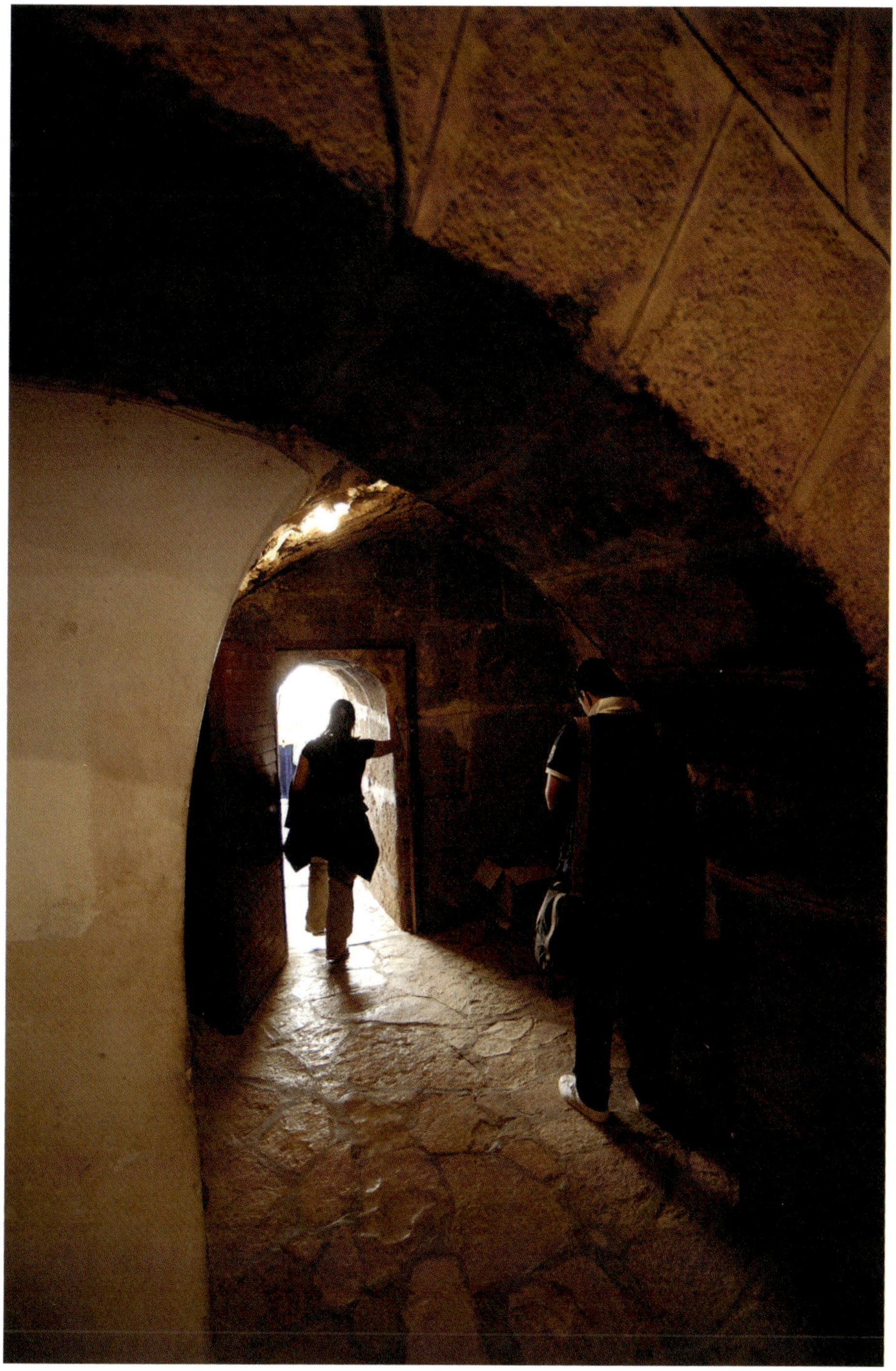

"The time that the people of Israel lived in Egypt was 430 years. At the end of 430 years, on that very day, all the hosts of the LORD went out from the land of Egypt. It was a night of watching by the LORD, to bring them out of the land of Egypt; so this same night is a night of watching kept to the LORD by all the people of Israel throughout their generations."

– Exodus 12:40-42 (ESV)

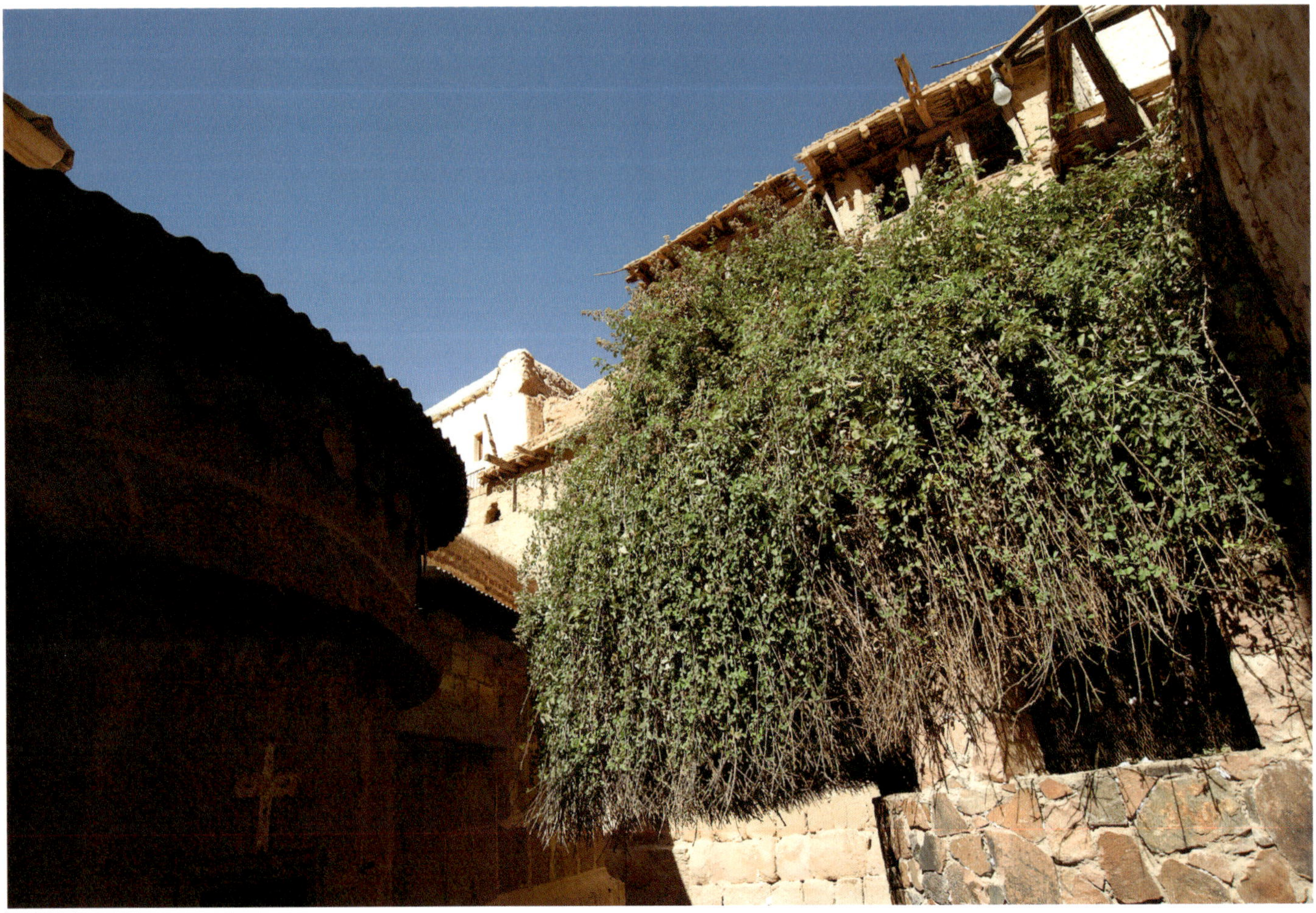

Above: **A bush in the courtyard of St. Catherine's Monastery**
This particular bush is held in monastic tradition to be *the* burning bush seen by Moses.

"'Do not come any closer,' God said. 'Take off your sandals, for the place where you are standing is holy ground.' Then he said, 'I am the God of your father, the God of Abraham, the God of Isaac and the God of Jacob.' At this, Moses hid his face, because he was afraid to look at God. The LORD said, 'I have indeed seen the misery of my people in Egypt. I have heard them crying out because of their slave drivers, and I am concerned about their suffering. So I have come down to rescue them from the hand of the Egyptians...'"

– Exodus 3:5-8 (NIV)

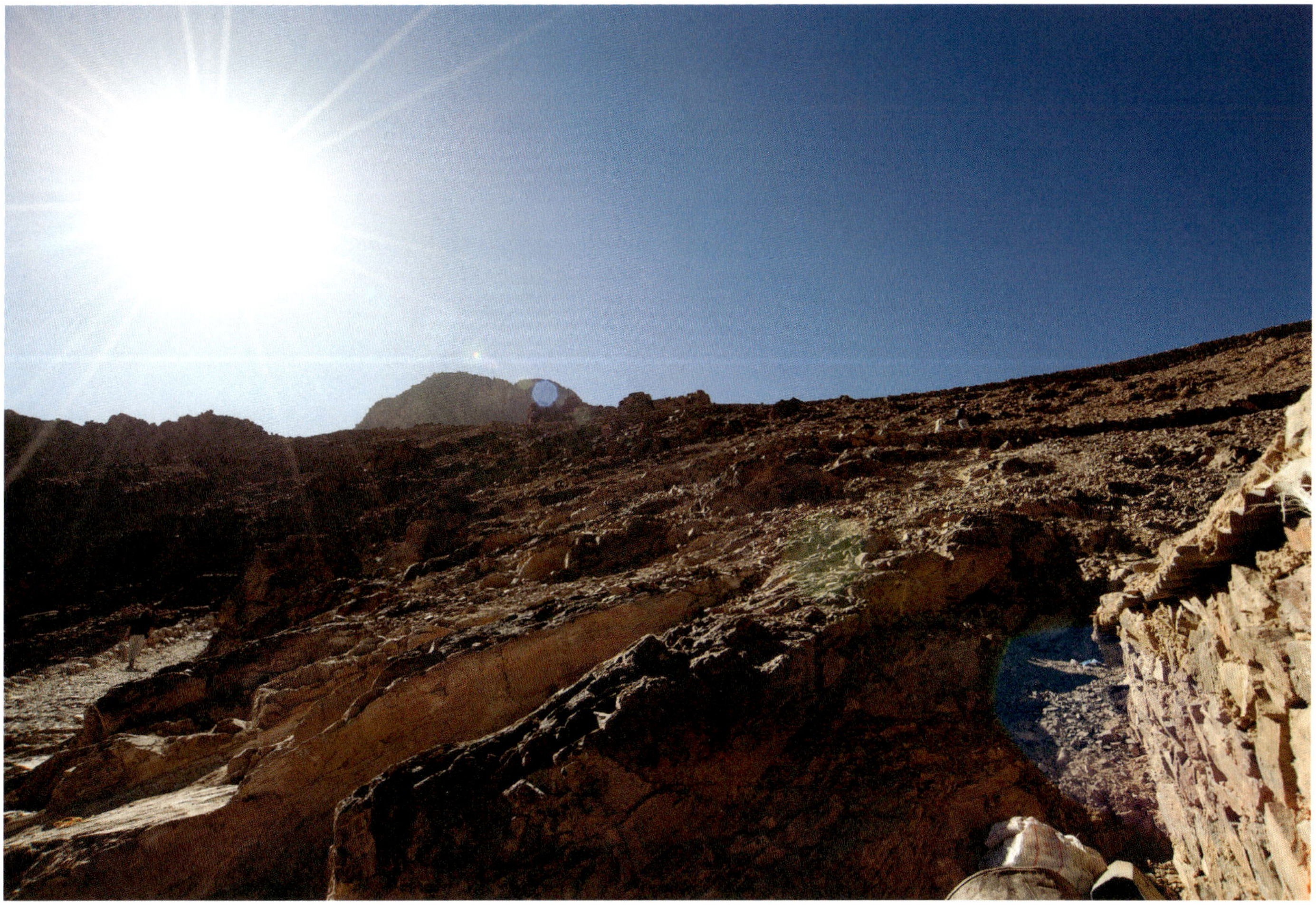

Pages 11-17: **Mount Sinai, Egypt**

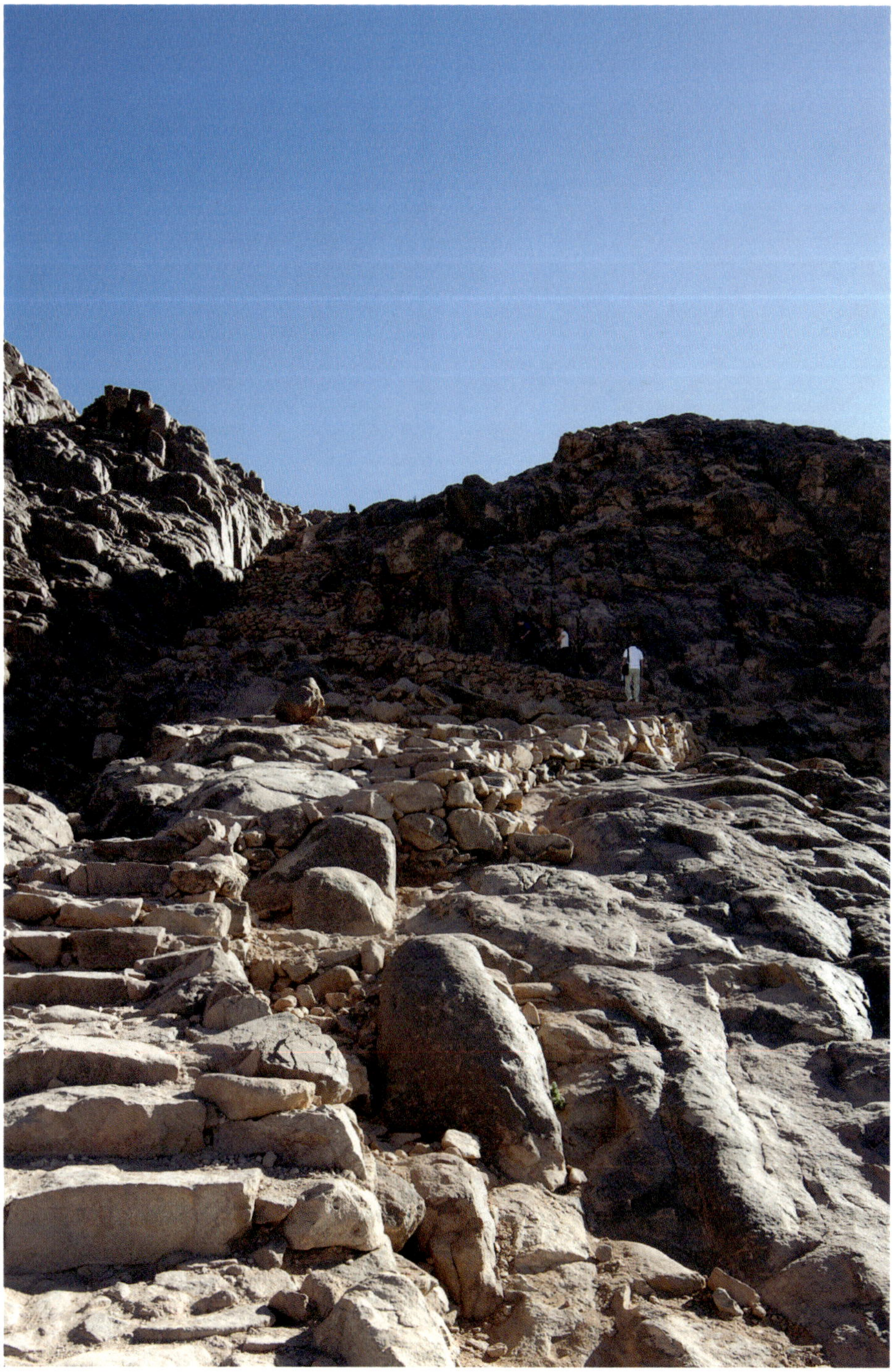

“After they set out from Rephidim, they entered the Desert of Sinai, and Israel camped there in the desert in front of the mountain. Then Moses went up to God, and the LORD called to him from the mountain and said, 'This is what you are to say to the house of Jacob and what you are to tell the people of Israel: 'You yourselves have seen what I did to Egypt, and how I carried you on eagles' wings and brought you to myself. Now if you

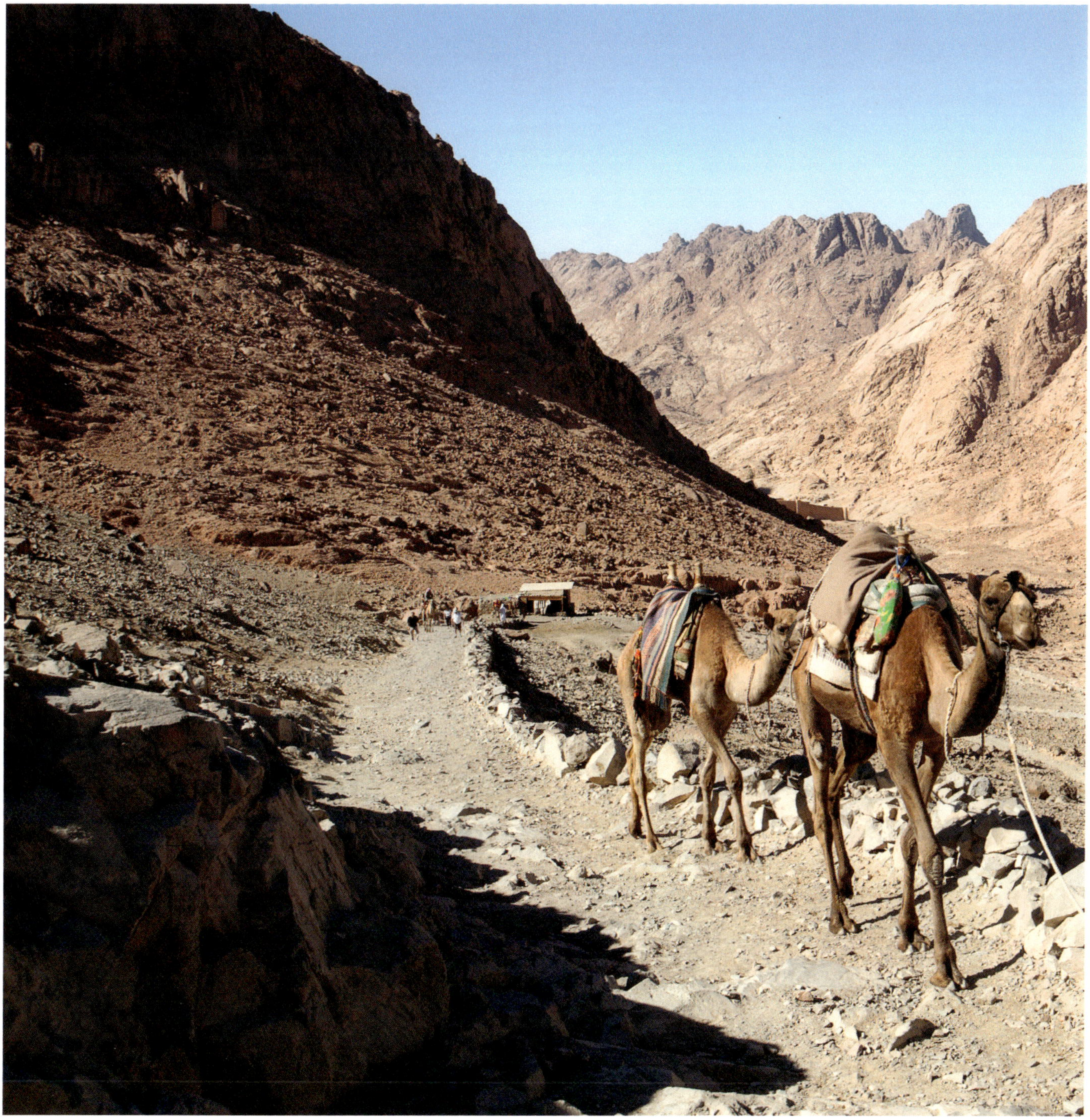

obey me fully and keep my covenant, then out of all nations you will be my treasured possession. Although the whole earth is mine, you will be for me a kingdom of priests and a holy nation.' These are the words you are to speak to the Israelites."'

– Exodus 19:2-6 (NIV)

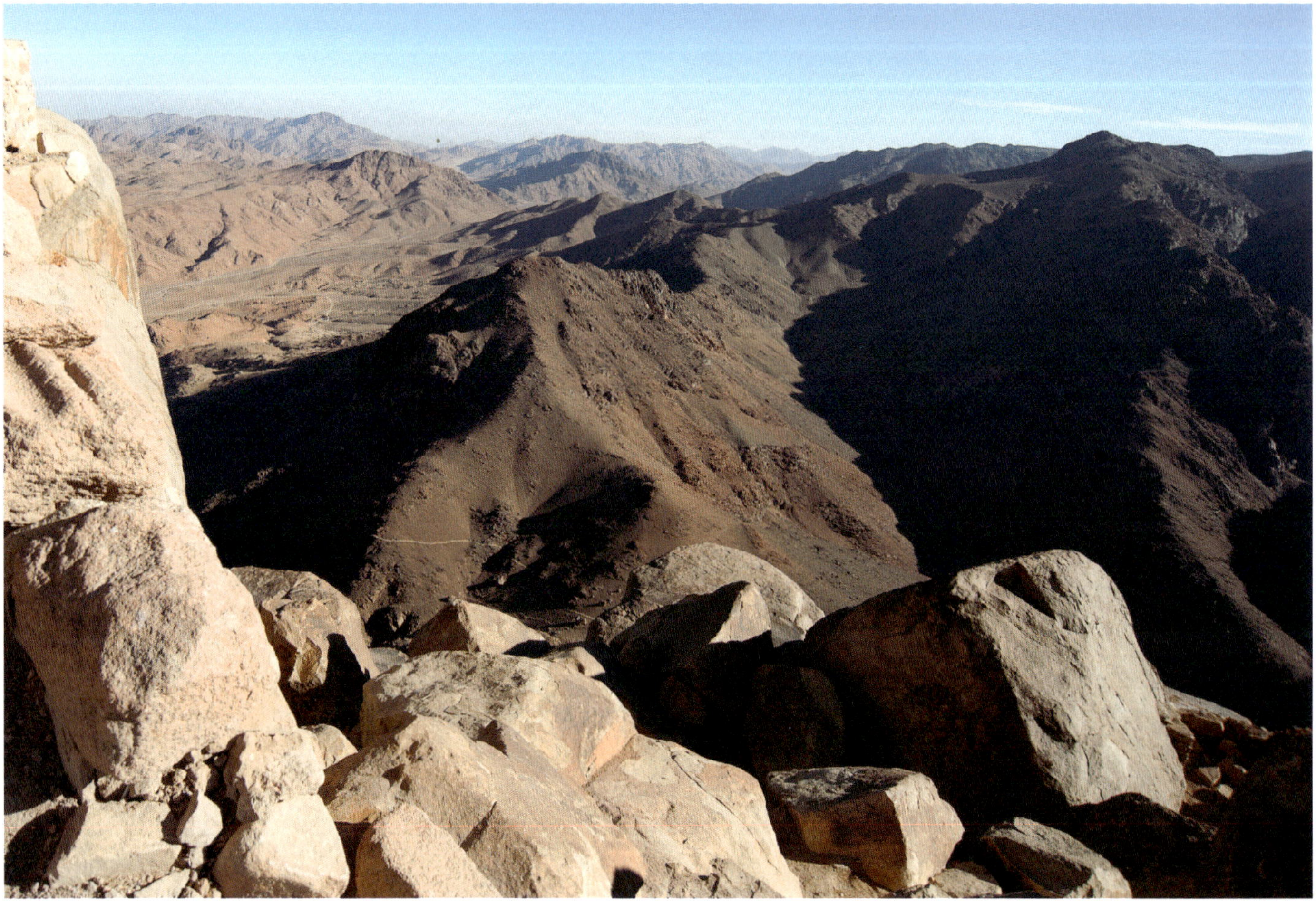

"On the morning of the third day there were thunders and lightnings and a thick cloud on the mountain and a very loud trumpet blast, so that all the people in the camp trembled. Then Moses brought the people out of the camp to meet God, and they took their stand at the foot of the mountain. Now Mount Sinai was wrapped in smoke because the LORD had descended on it in fire. The smoke of it went up like the smoke of a kiln, and the whole mountain trembled greatly. And as the sound of the trumpet grew louder and louder, Moses spoke, and God answered him in thunder. The LORD came down on Mount Sinai, to the top of the mountain. And the LORD called Moses to the top of the mountain, and Moses went up."

– Exodus 19:16-20 (ESV)

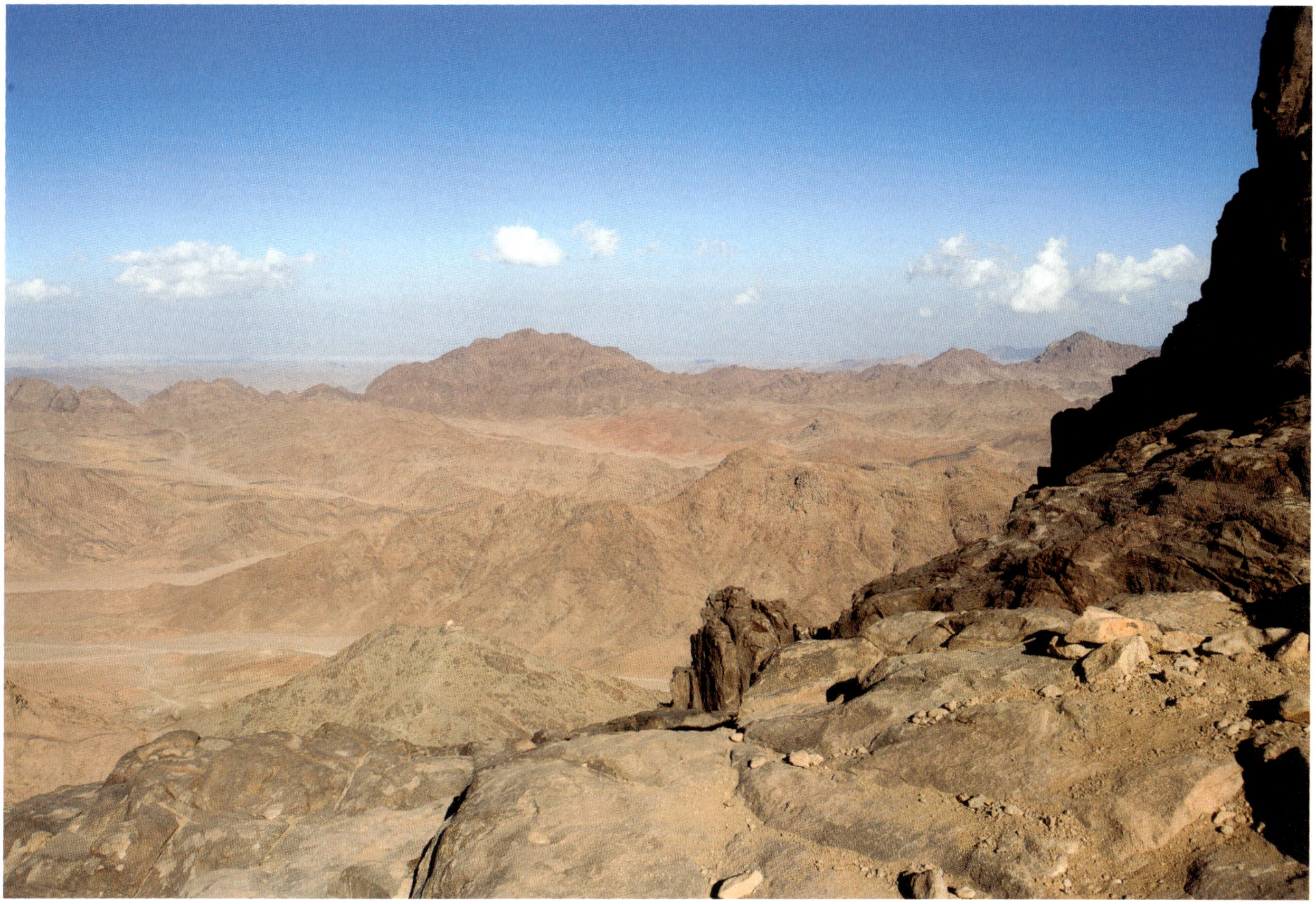

"When Moses came down from Mount Sinai, with the two tablets of the testimony in his hand as he came down from the mountain, Moses did not know that the skin of his face shone because he had been talking with God. Aaron and all the people of Israel saw Moses, and behold, the skin of his face shone, and they were afraid to come near him. But Moses called to them, and Aaron and all the leaders of the congregation returned to him, and Moses talked with them. Afterward all the people of Israel came near, and he commanded them all that the LORD had spoken with him in Mount Sinai."

– Exodus 34:29-32 (ESV)

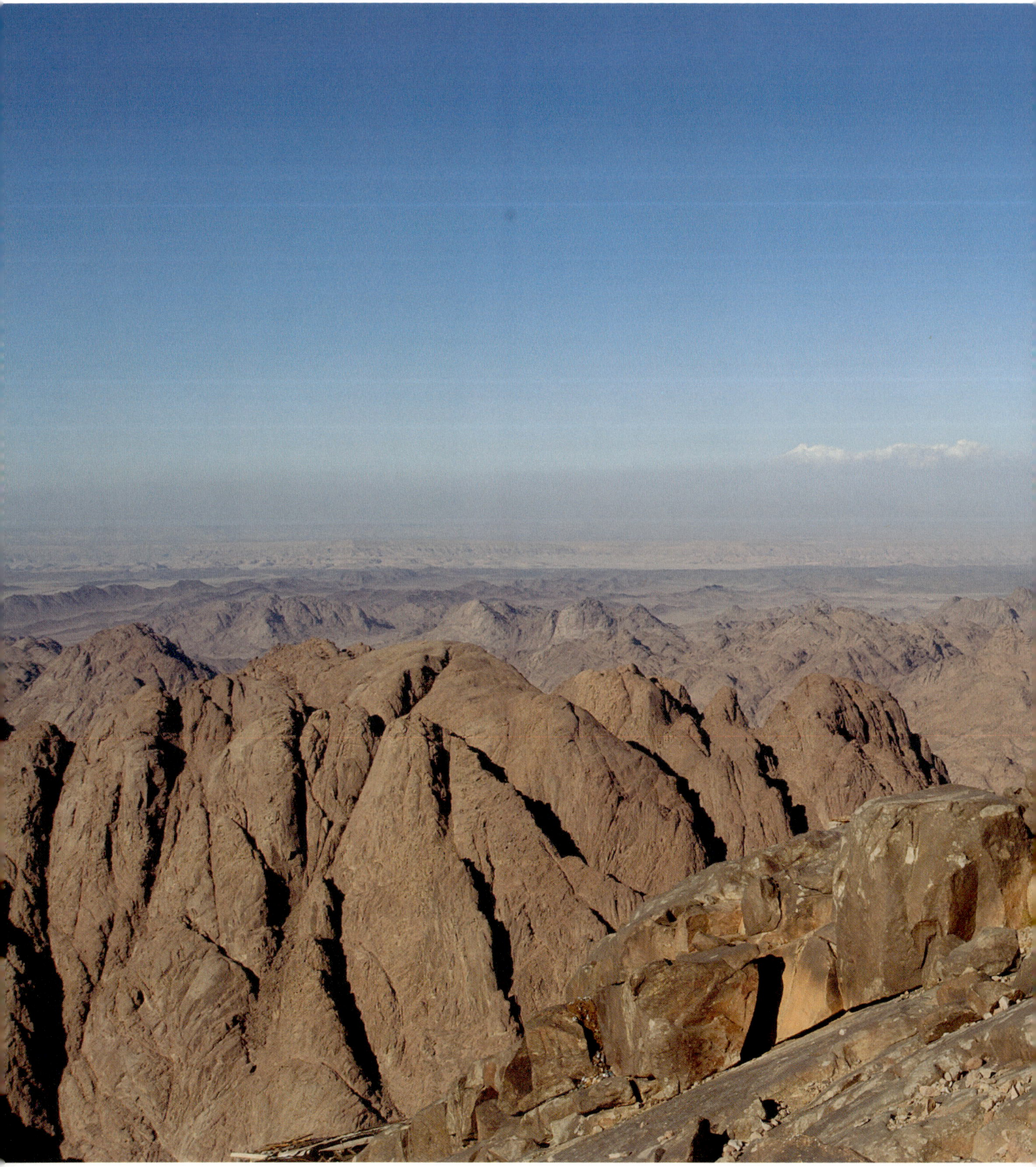

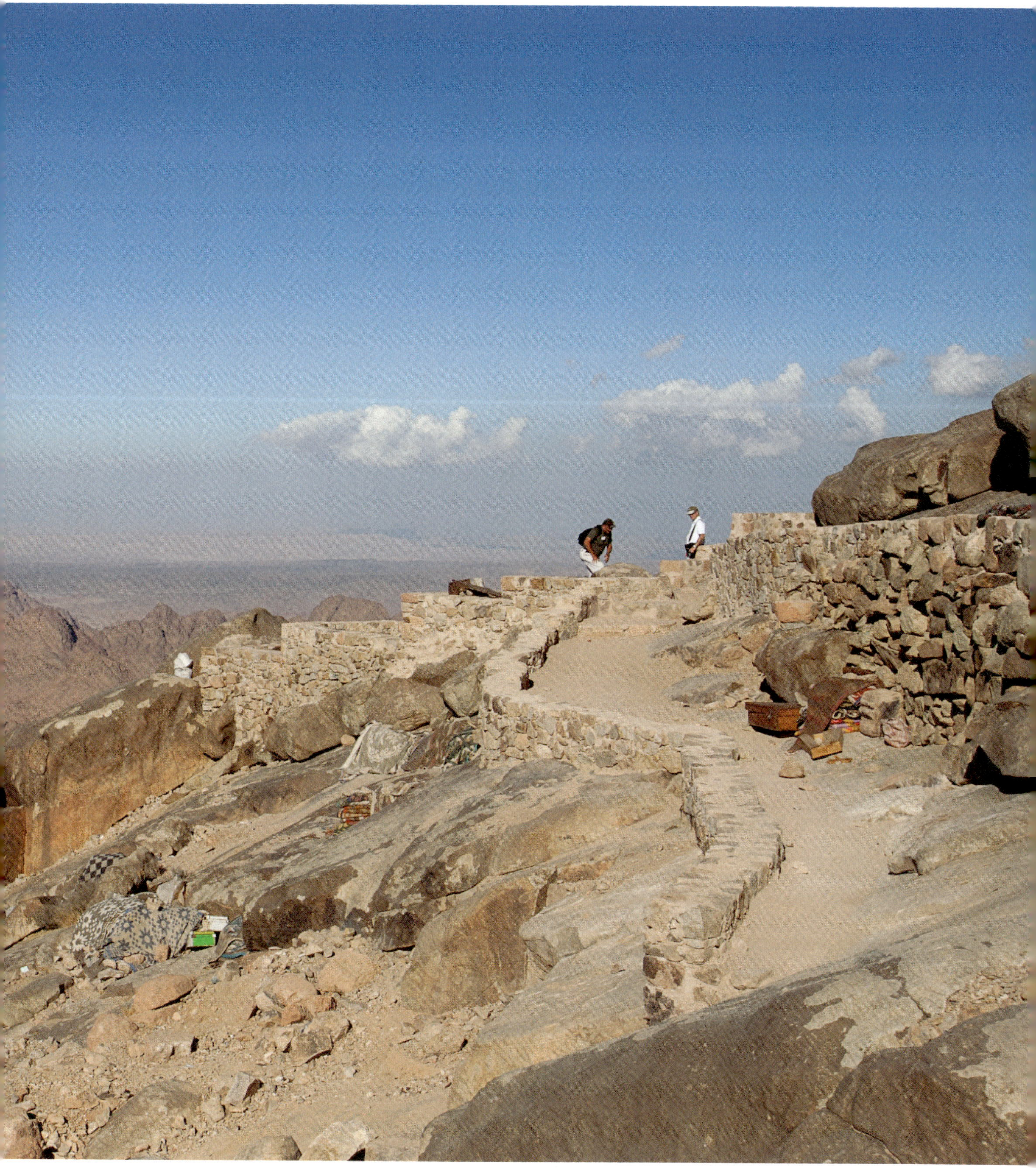

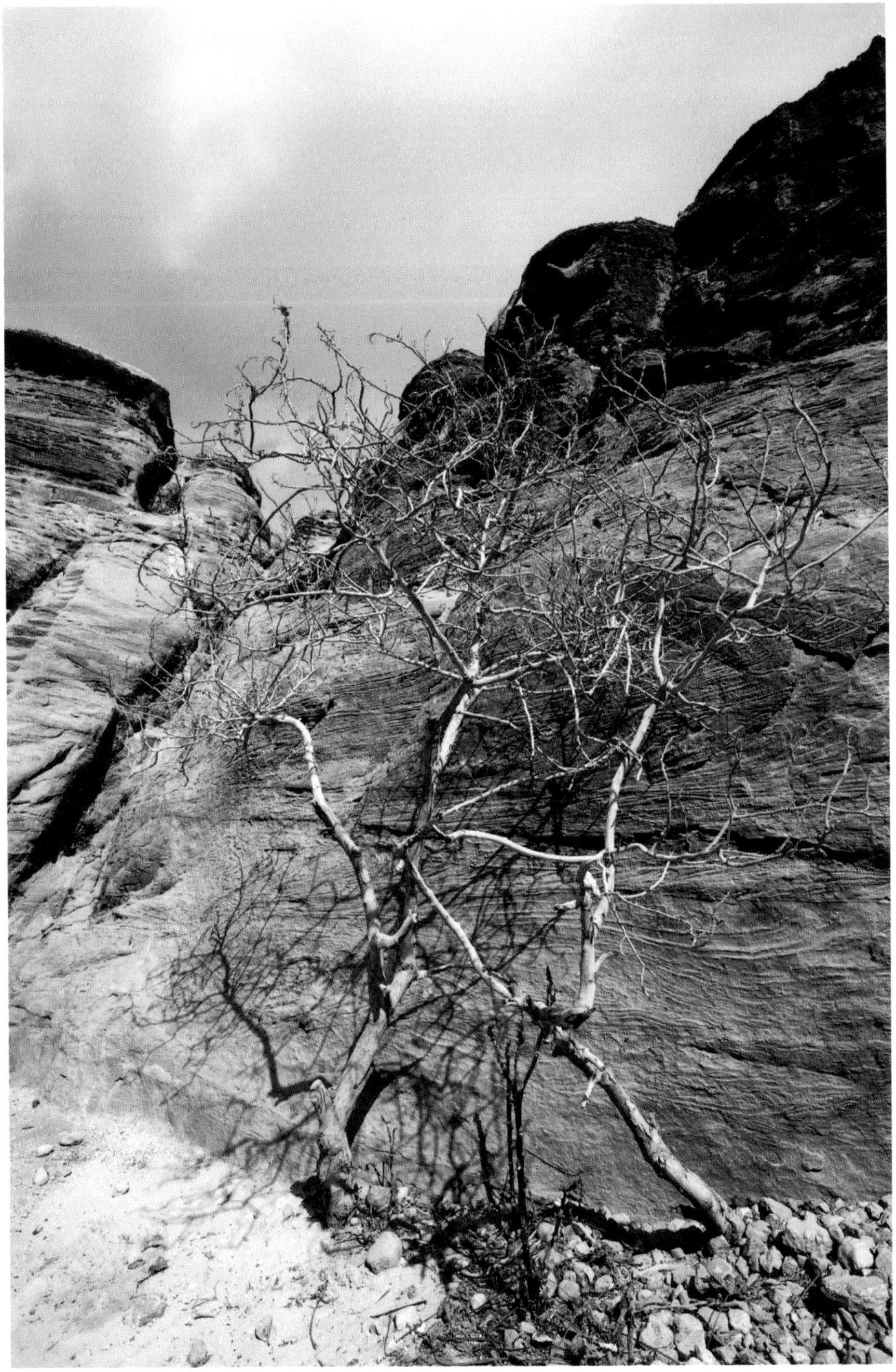

"...as surely as I live and as surely as the glory of the LORD fills the whole earth, not one of those who saw my glory and the signs I performed in Egypt and in the wilderness but who disobeyed Me and tested Me ten times – not one of them will ever see the land I promised on oath to their forefathers. No one who has treated Me with contempt will ever see it. But because my servant Caleb has a different spirit and follows Me wholeheartedly, I will bring him into the land he went to, and his descendants will inherit it. Since the Amalekites and Canaanites are living in the valleys, turn back tomorrow and set out toward the desert along the route to the Red Sea."

– Numbers 14:21-25 (NIV)

Jordan

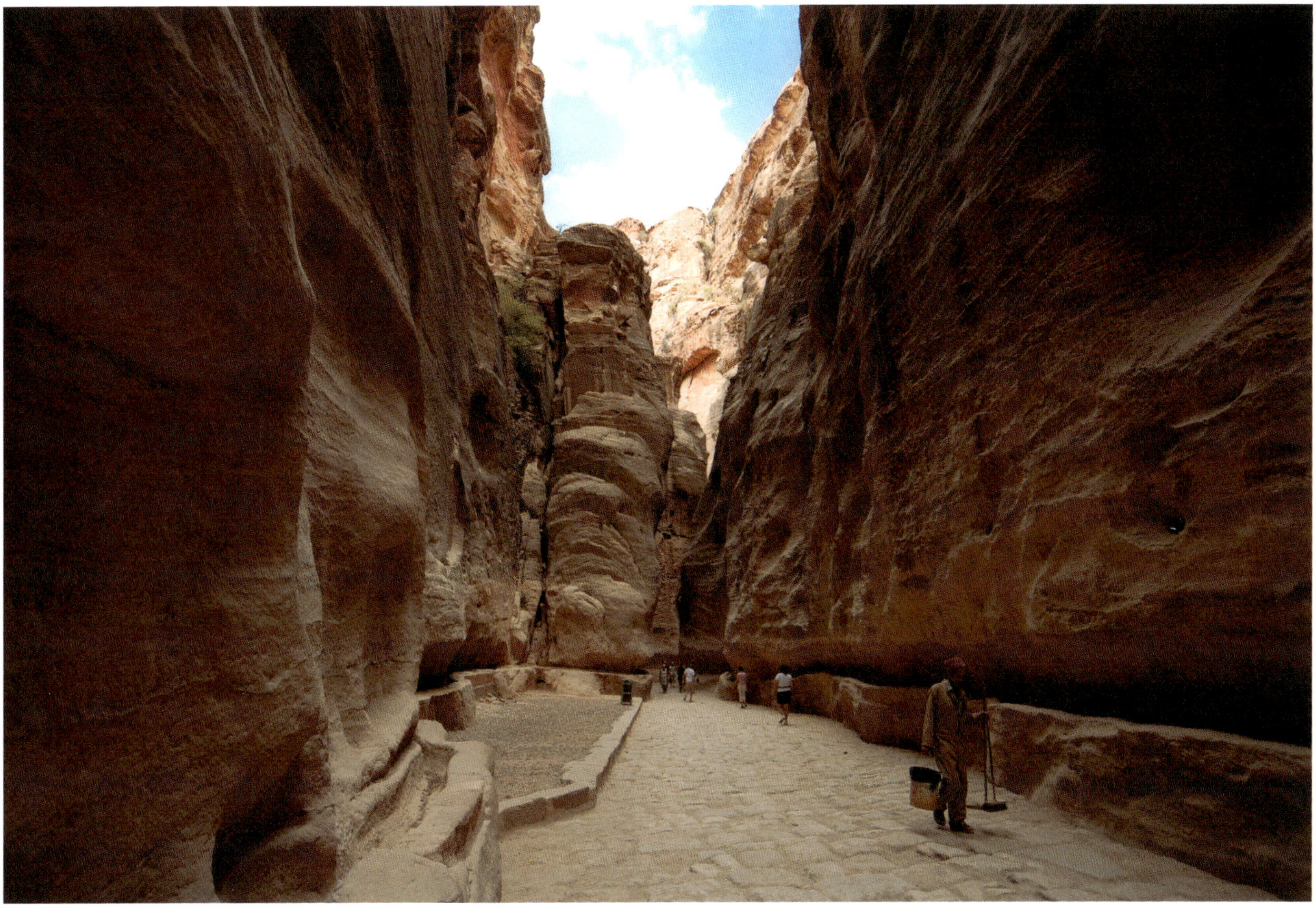

Left: **Jordanian desert at Petra, in the vicinity of modern-day Ma'an**

Pages 19-24: **Nabetean city of Petra**
This site lies in harsh terrain where the nation of Israel lived for forty years. The ruins here are carved into the side of Mount Hor, which is the biblical site of Aaron's death, but they are not contemporaneous with the Exodus (around 1400 B.C.). The city dates from around 600 B.C. to the late Roman period, approximately 700 A.D.

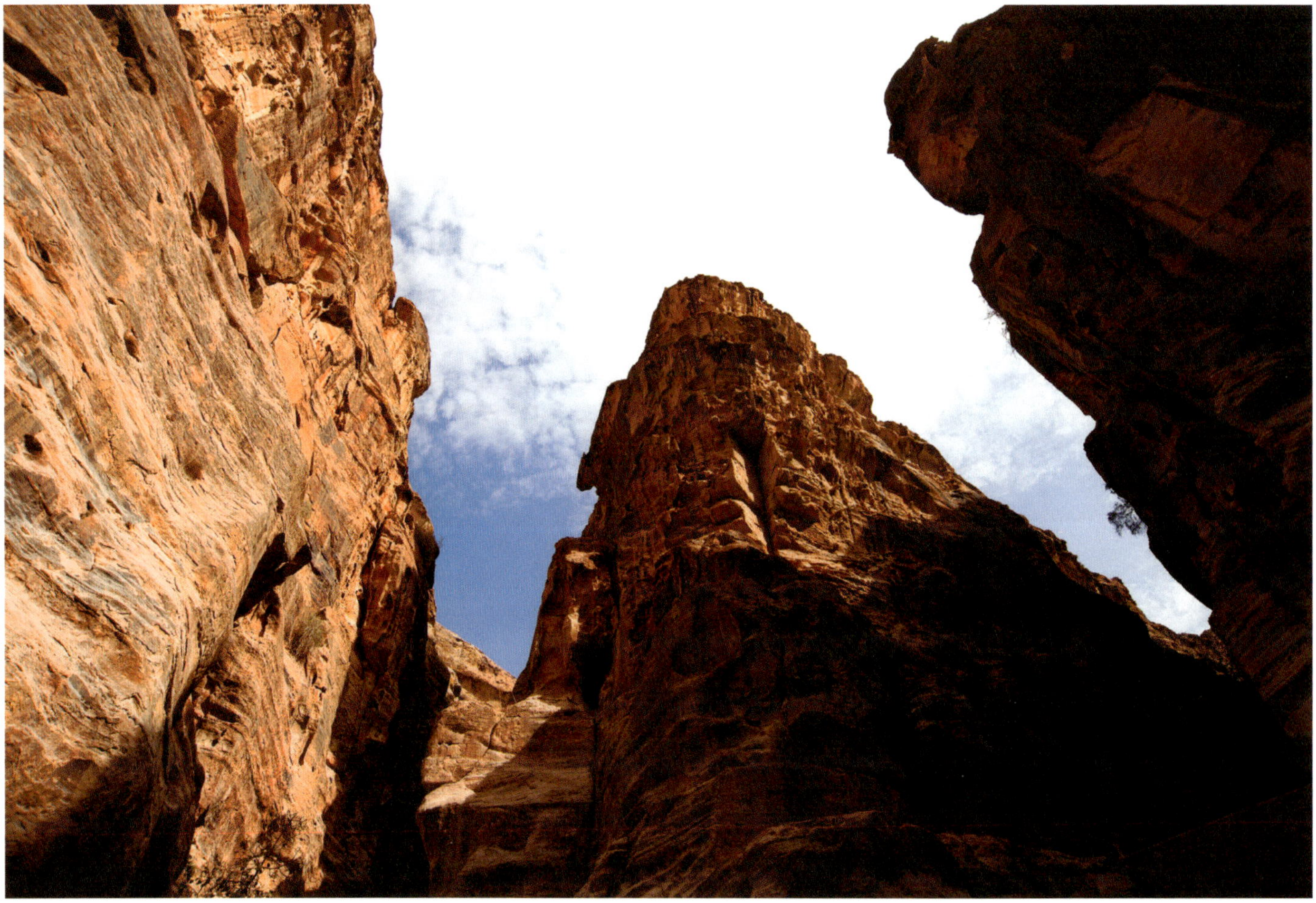

"The whole Israelite community set out from Kadesh and came to Mount Hor. At Mount Hor, near the border of Edom, the LORD said to Moses and Aaron, 'Aaron will be gathered to his people. He will not enter the land I give the Israelites, because both of you rebelled against my command at the waters of Meribah. Get Aaron and his son Eleazar and take them up Mount Hor. Remove Aaron's garments and put them on his son Eleazar, for Aaron will be gathered to his people; he will die there.' Moses did as the LORD commanded: They went up Mount Hor in the sight of the whole community. Moses removed Aaron's garments and put them on his son Eleazar. And Aaron died there on top of the mountain. Then Moses and Eleazar came down from the mountain, and when the whole community learned that Aaron had died, the entire house of Israel mourned for him thirty days."

– Numbers 20:22-29 (NIV)

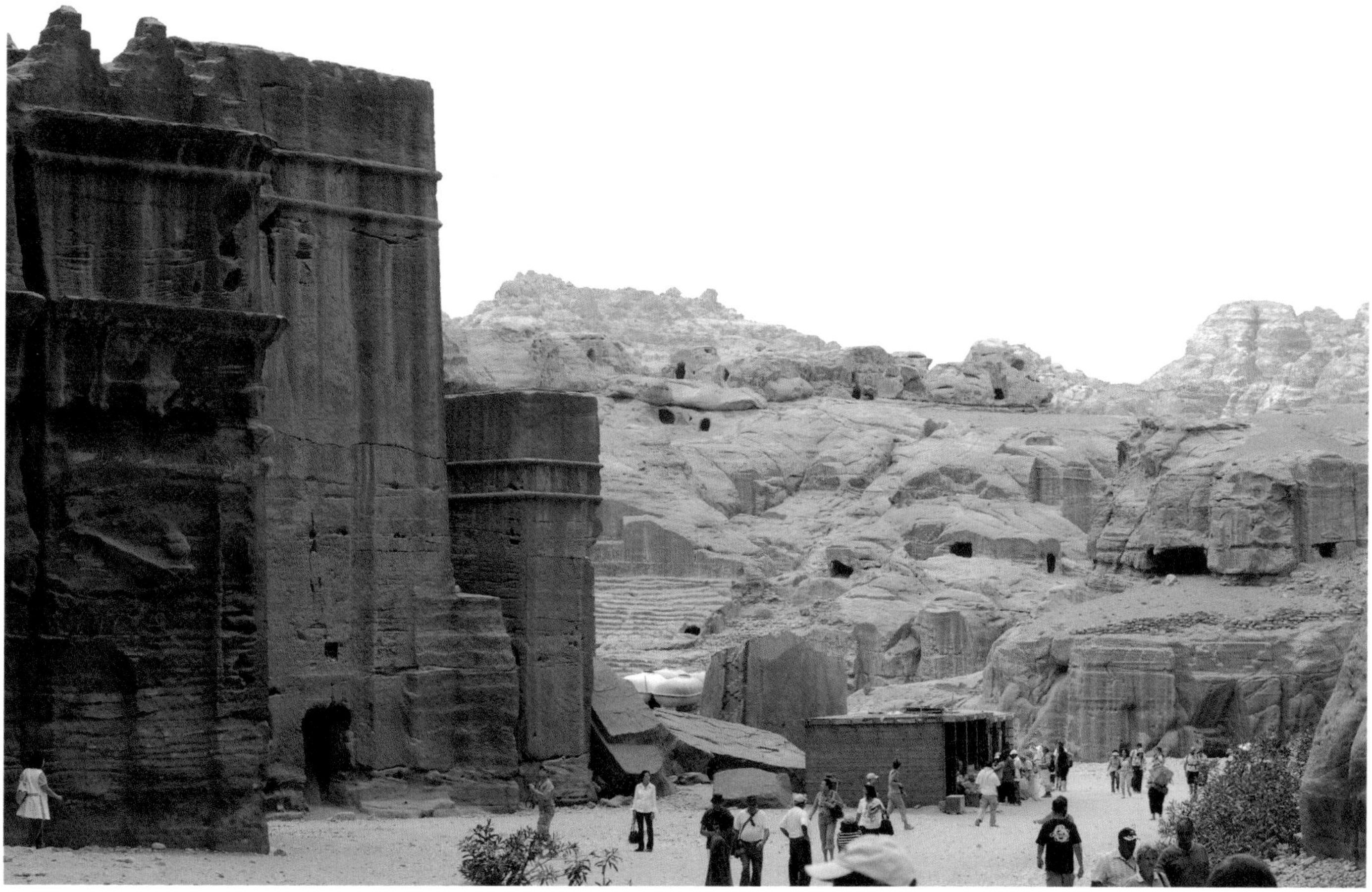

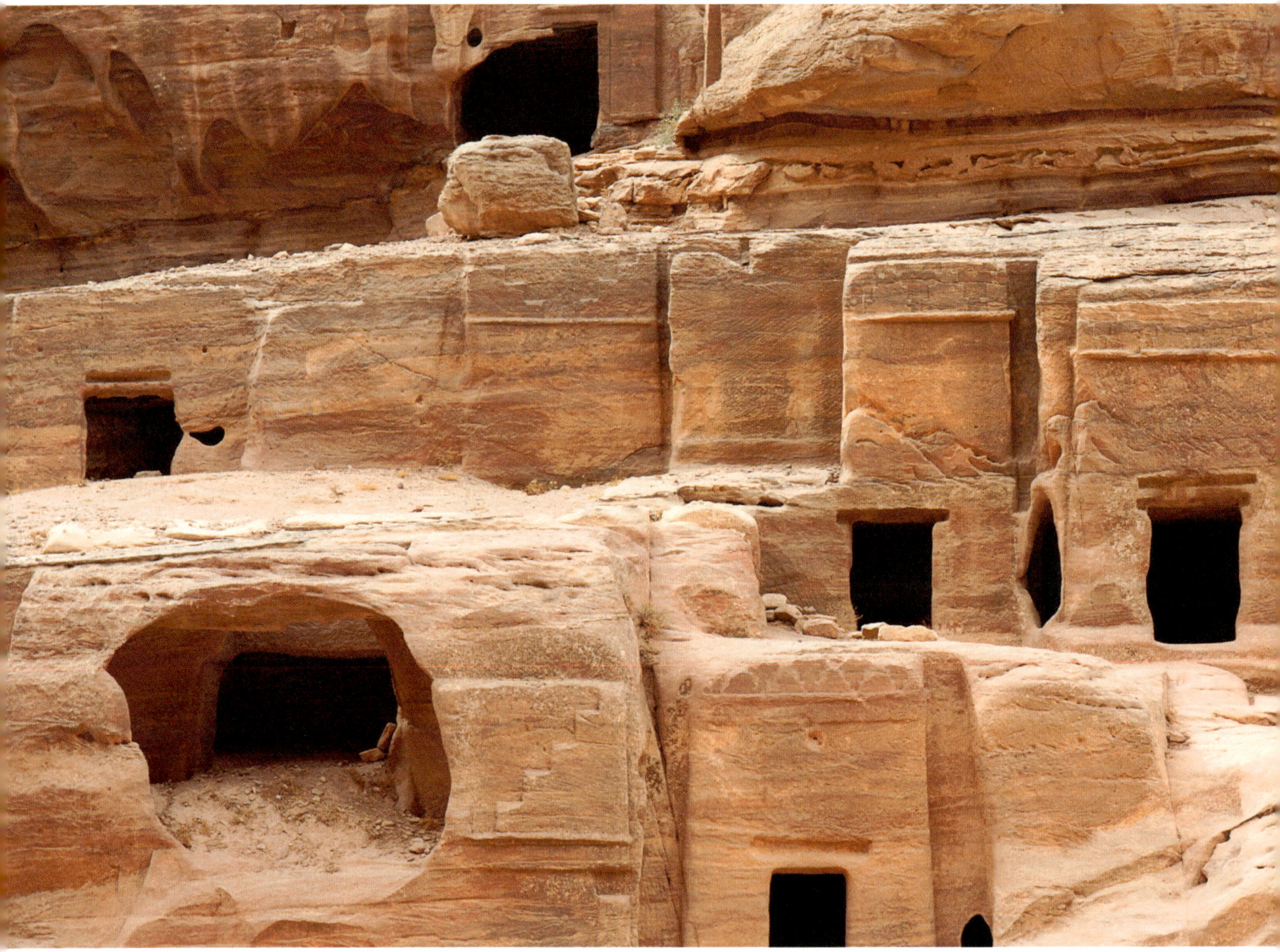

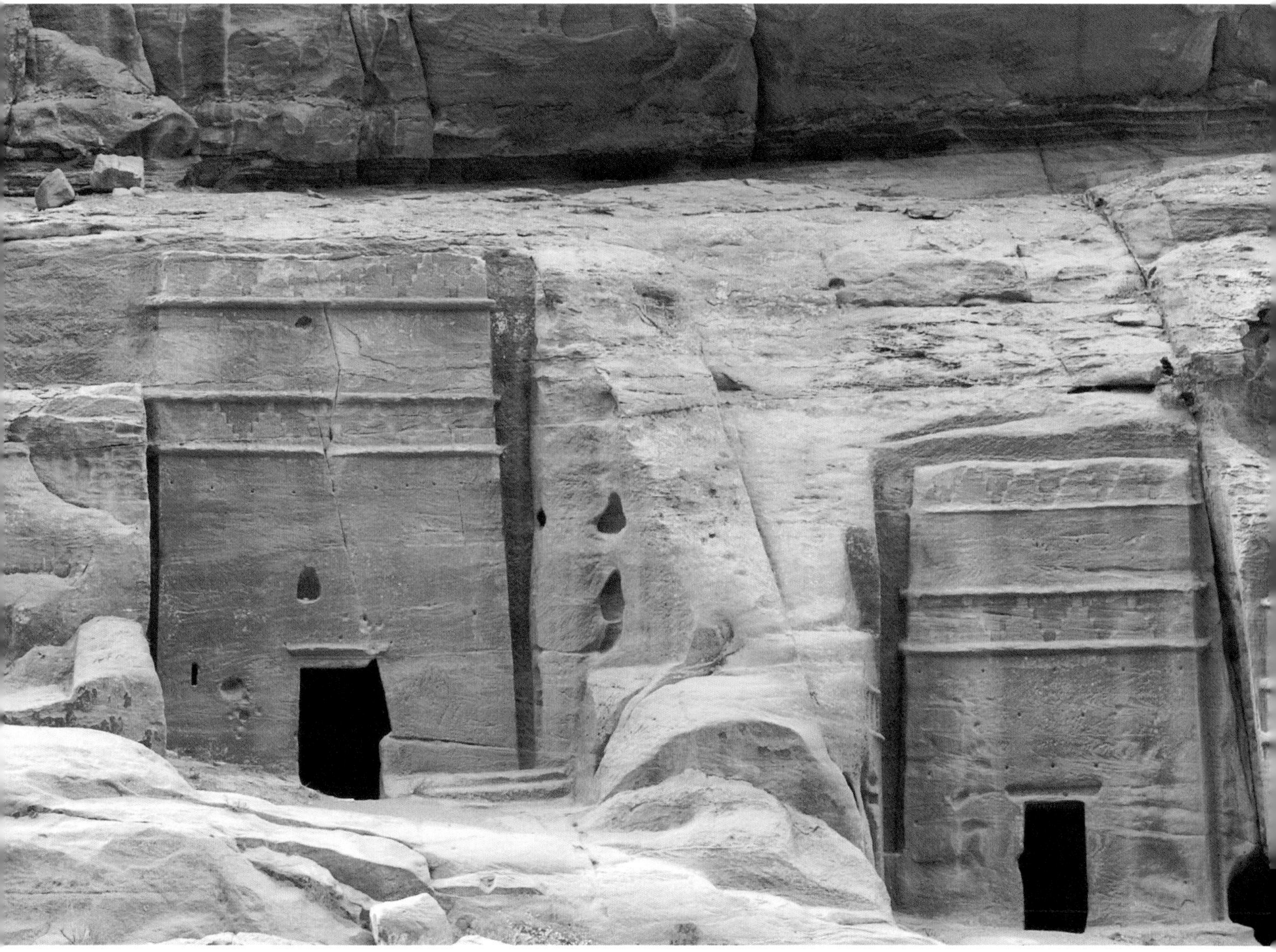

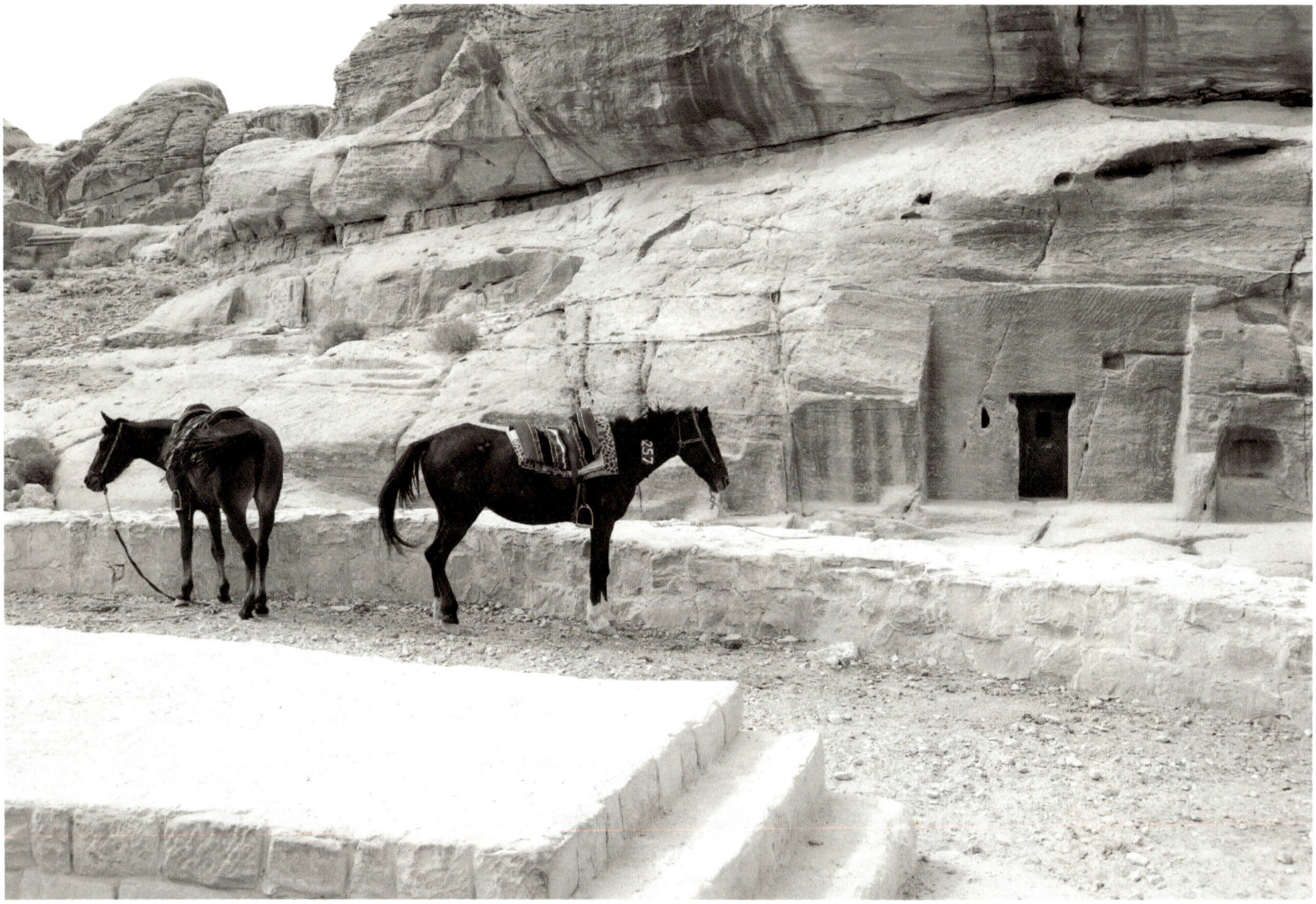

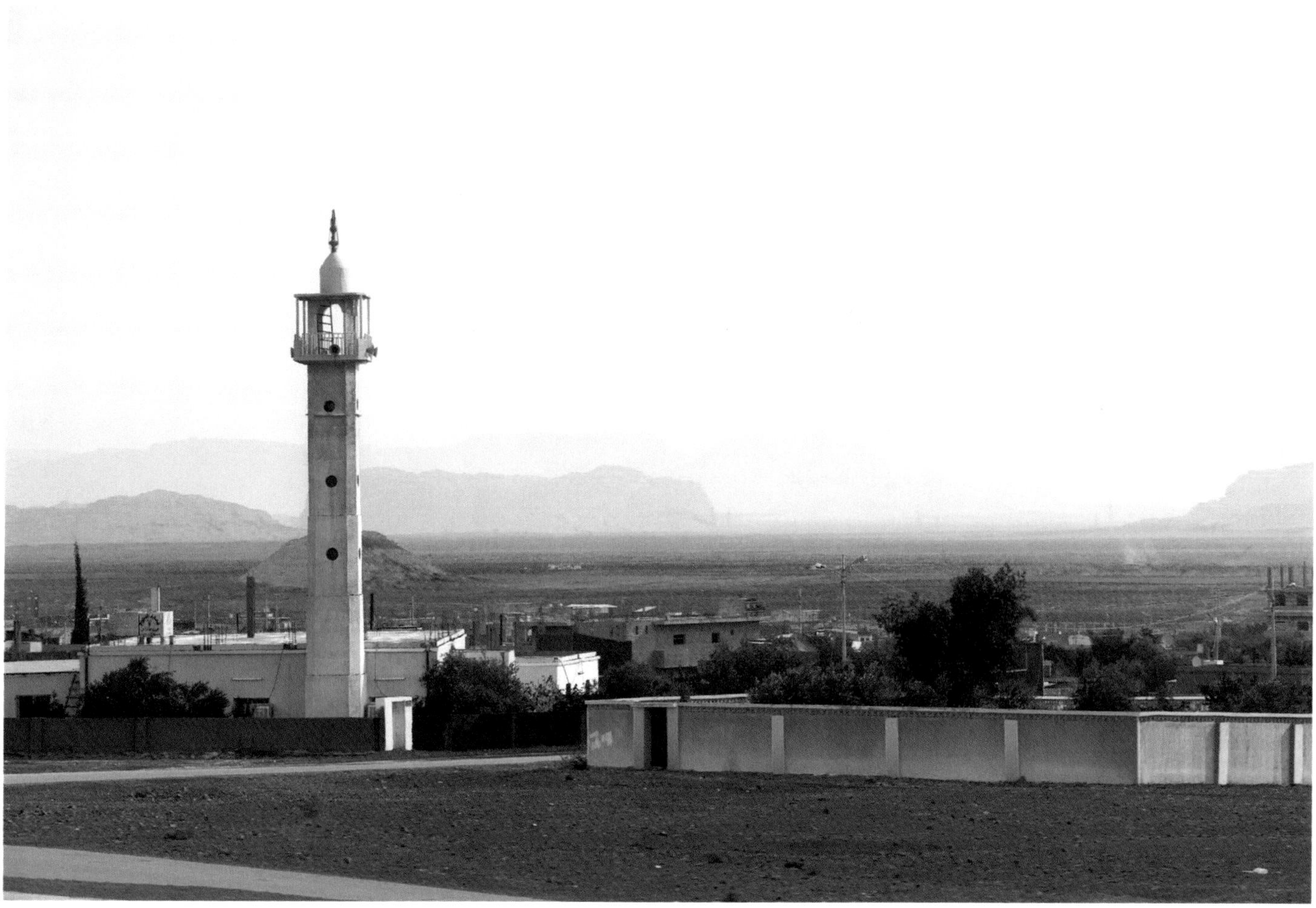

Above: **A minaret and small village in the Jordanian desert**

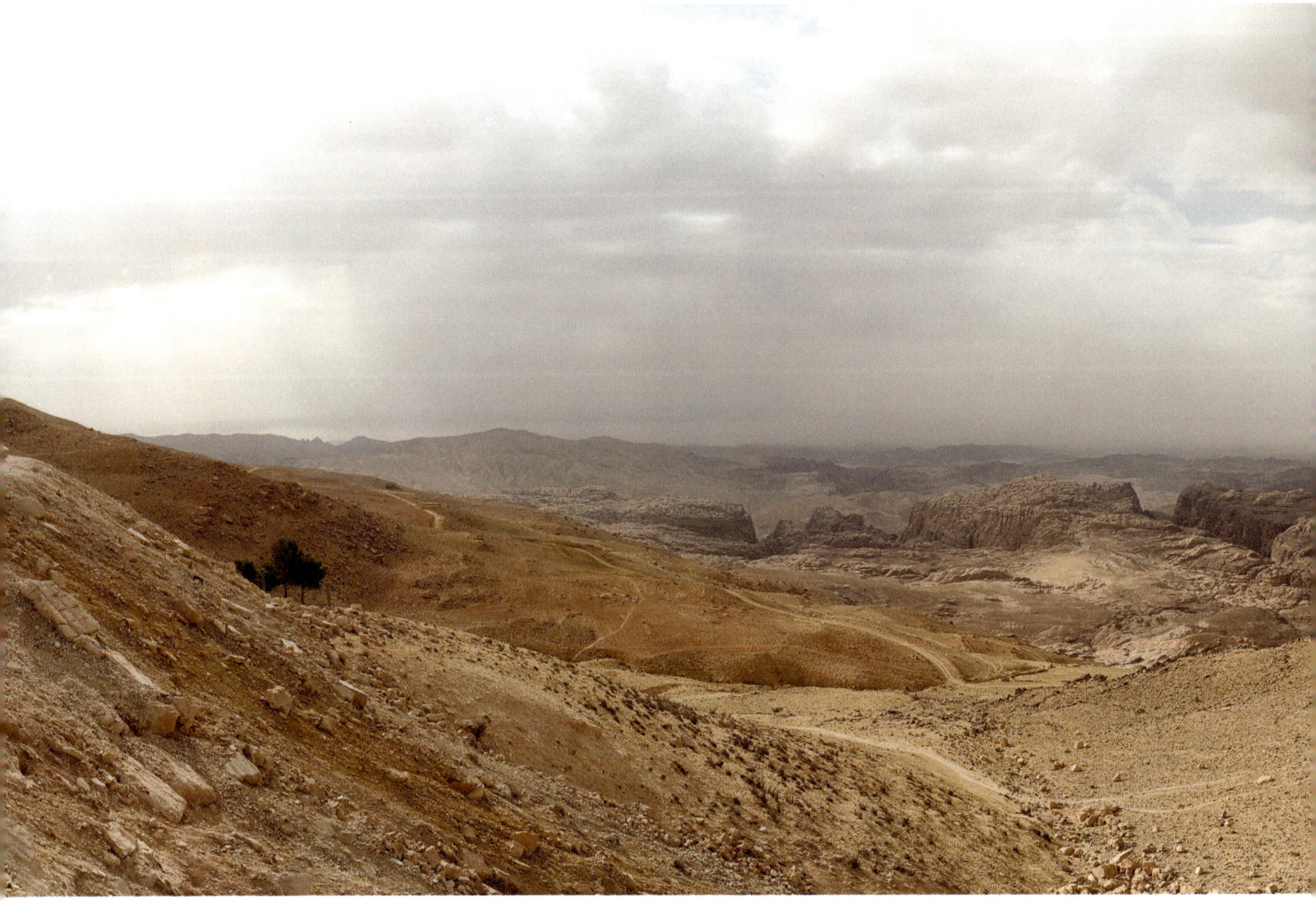

"And when all these things come upon you, the blessing and the curse, which I have set before you, and you call them to mind among all the nations where the LORD your God has driven you, and return to the LORD your God, you and your children, and obey His voice in all that I command you today, with all your heart and with all your soul, then the LORD your God will restore your fortunes and have compassion on you, and He will gather you again from all the peoples where the LORD your God has scattered

Below: **The Hills of Aaron**
Mount Hor is in the center-right of the picture. The view points towards Israel, about 15 miles away. At the time of the Exodus, this area would have been on the borders of the biblical nation Edom.

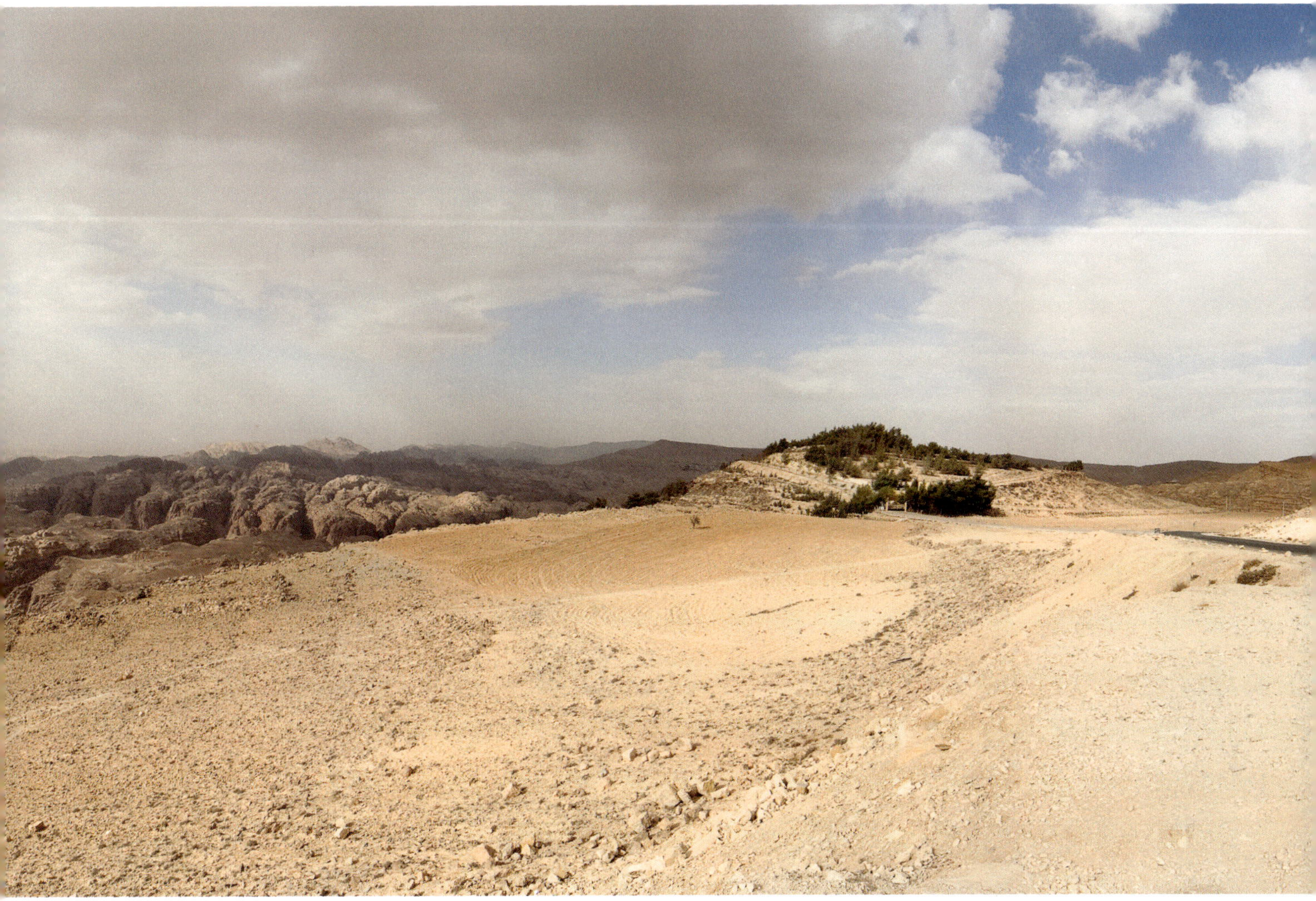

you. If your outcasts are in the uttermost parts of heaven, from there the LORD your God will gather you, and from there He will take you. And the LORD your God will bring you into the land that your fathers possessed, that you may possess it. And He will make you more prosperous and numerous than your fathers. And the LORD your God will circumcise your heart and the heart of your offspring, so that you will love the LORD your God with all your heart and with all your soul, that you may live."

– Deuteronomy 30:1-6 (ESV)

"The LORD is my shepherd; I shall not want.

He maketh me to lie down in green pastures: He leadeth me beside the still waters.

He restoreth my soul: He leadeth me in the paths of righteousness for his name's sake.

Yea, though I walk through the valley of the shadow of death, I will fear no evil: for Thou art with me; Thy rod and Thy staff they comfort me.

Thou preparest a table before me in the presence of mine enemies: Thou anointest my head with oil; my cup runneth over.

Surely goodness and mercy shall follow me all the days of my life: and I will dwell in the house of the LORD for ever."

– Psalm 23 (KJV)

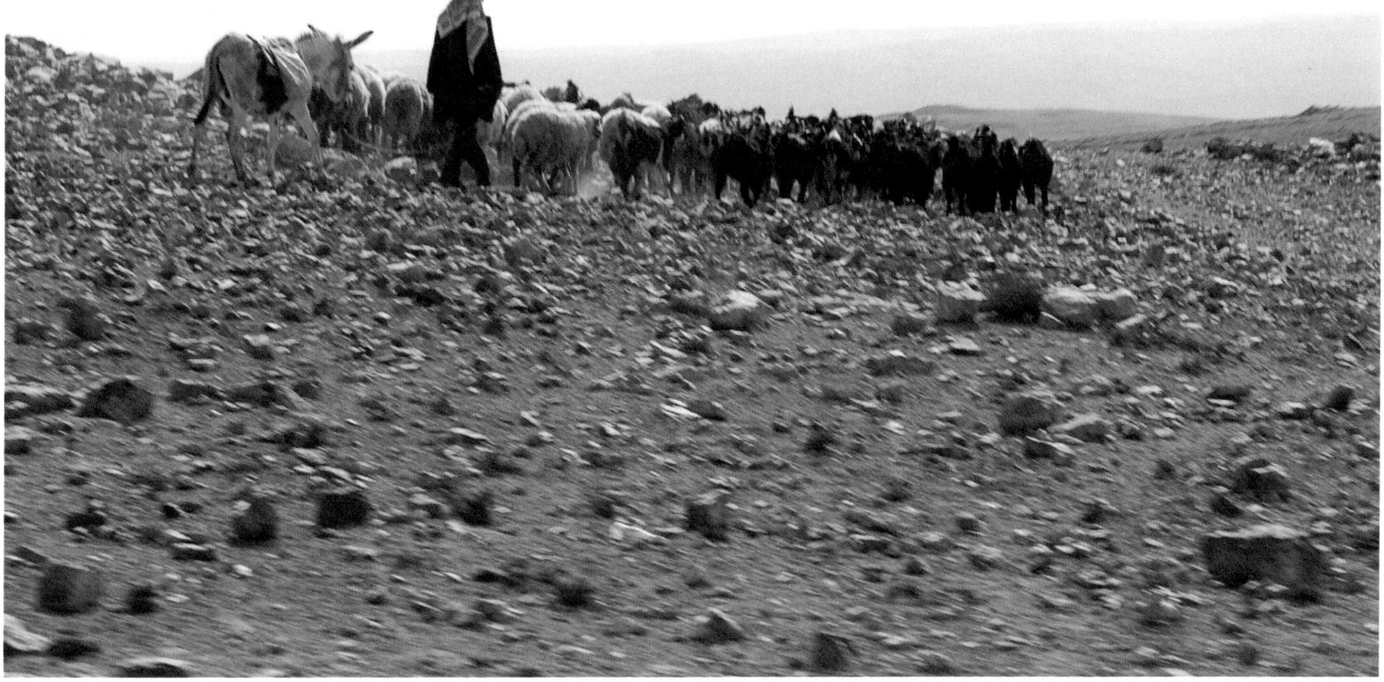

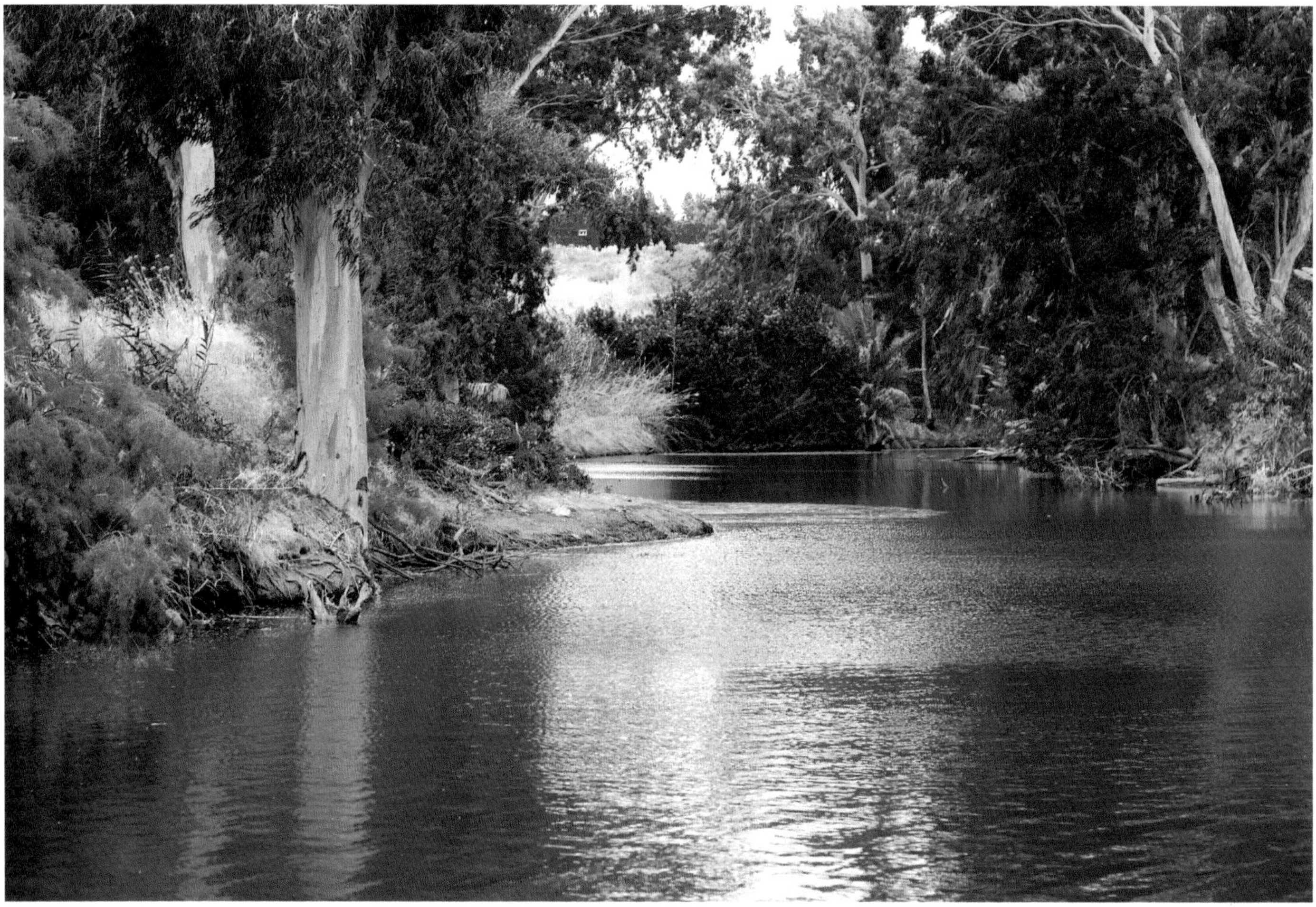

Above: **The Jordan River**
The Israelites crossed into Israel several miles south of this point at Jericho.

On Jordan's stormy banks I stand,
And cast a wishful eye
To Canaan's fair and happy land,
Where my possessions lie.

No chilling winds or poisonous breath
Can reach that healthful shore;
Sickness and sorrow, pain and death,
Are felt and feared no more.

Israel

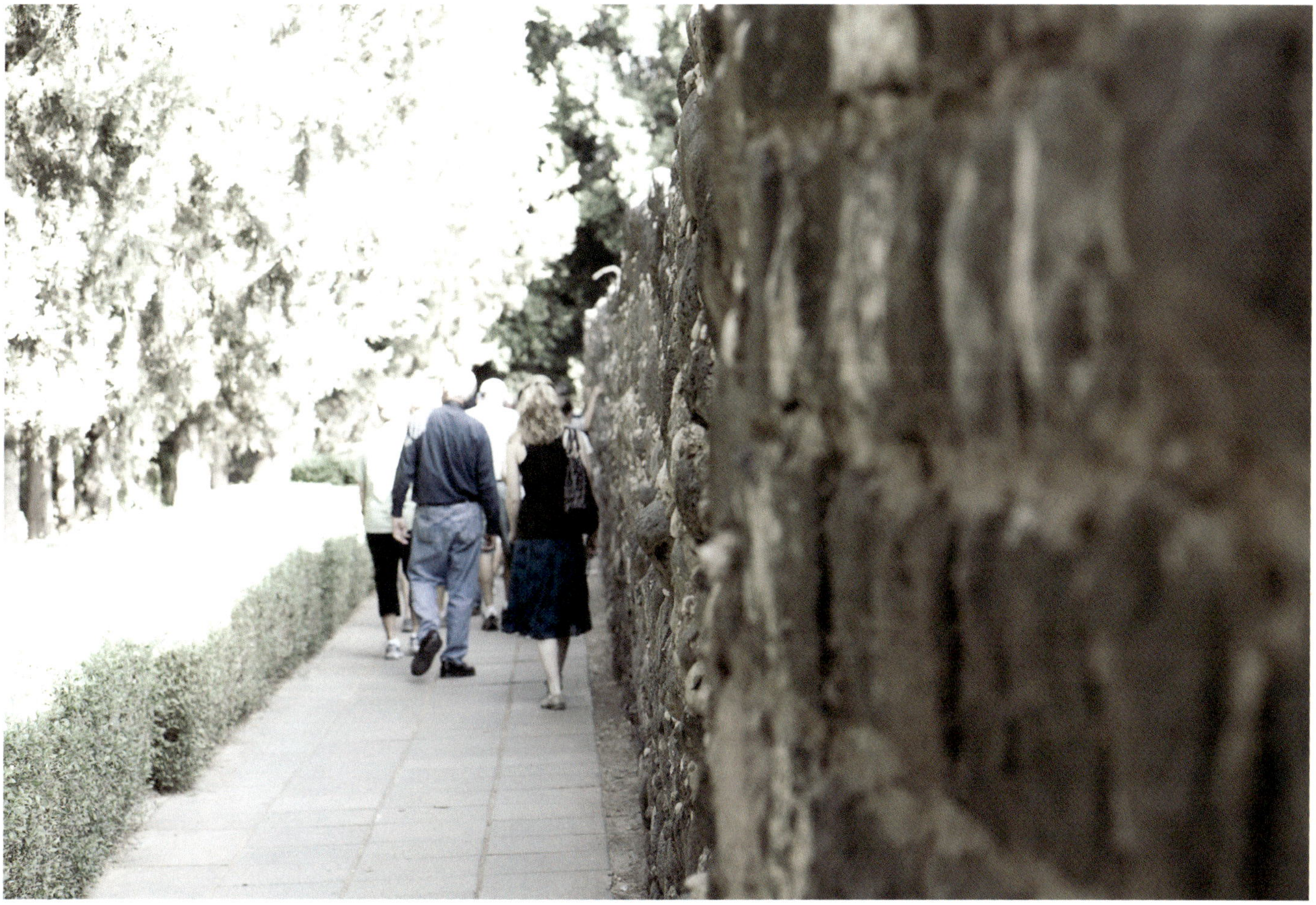

When I shall reach that happy place,
I'll be forever blest,
For I shall see my Father's face,
And in His bosom rest.

Filled with delight my raptured soul
Would here no longer stay;
Though Jordan's waves around me roll,
Fearless I'd launch away.

"On Jordan's Stormy Banks I Stand"
Verses 1, 5-7
Words by Samuel Stennett (1787)

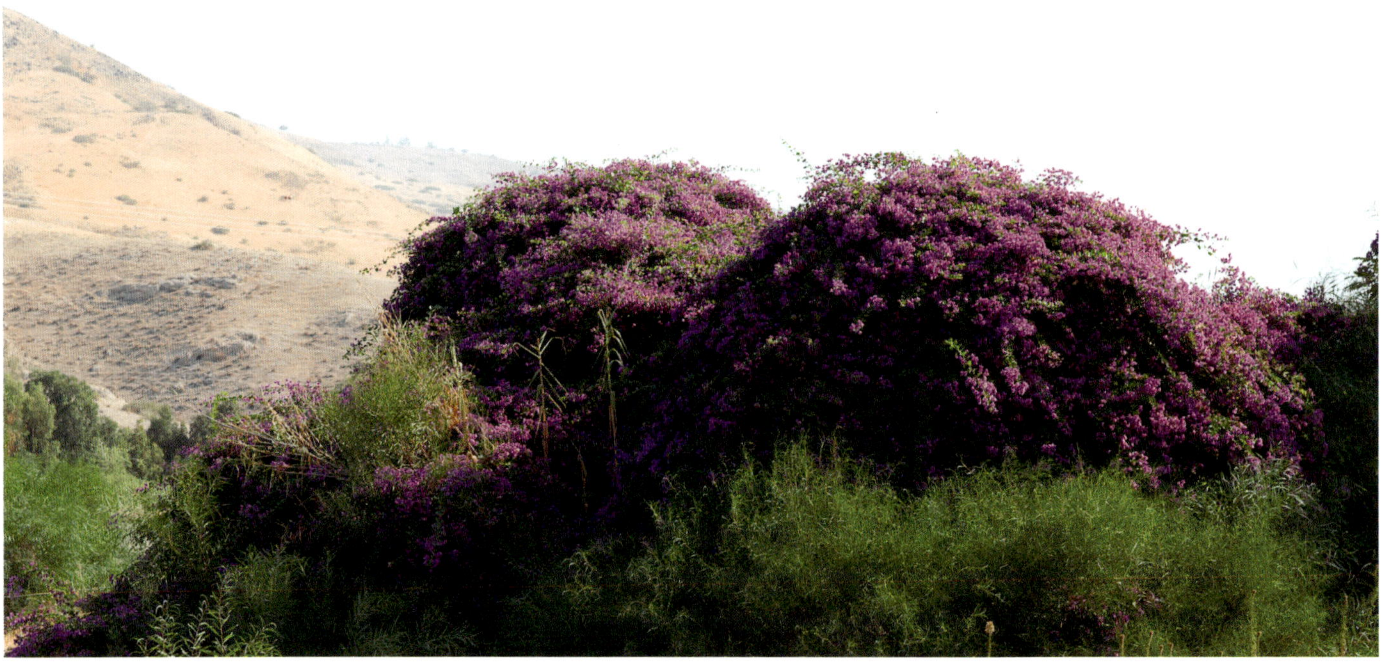

Above: **A rose of Sharon tree in northern Israel**
The Golan Heights are in the background.

"...you are a people holy to the LORD your God. The LORD your God has chosen you to be a people for His treasured possession, out of all the peoples who are on the face of the earth. It was not because you were more in number than any other people that the LORD set His love on you and chose you, for you were the fewest of all peoples, but it is because the LORD loves you and is keeping the oath that He swore to your fathers, that the LORD has brought you out with a mighty hand and redeemed you from the house of slavery, from the hand of Pharaoh king of Egypt."

– Deuteronomy 7:6-8 (ESV)

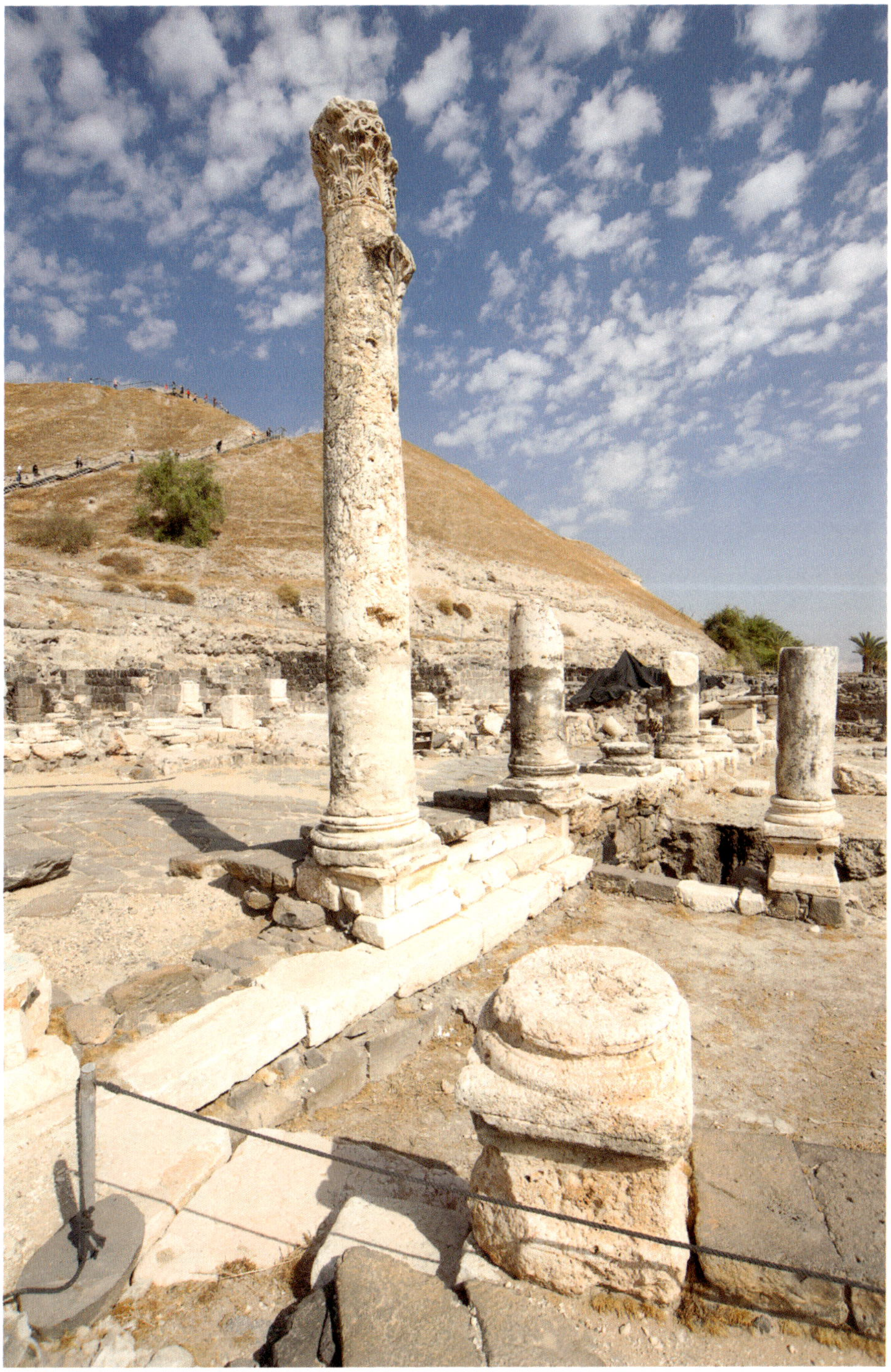

Pages 33-39: **Roman city of Scythopolis at Beit She'an**
Due to its strategic location along the Jordan river and trade routes to the East, this valley has been the site of many settlements. During the time of the Judges and the reign of Saul, the hill in the background was occupied first by Canaanites and then later was taken over by the Philistines. The Roman city existed in smaller form at the time of Jesus. It reached its zenith as the headquarters of the Sixth Legion in the second century A.D. and then was destroyed by earthquake in 749 A.D.

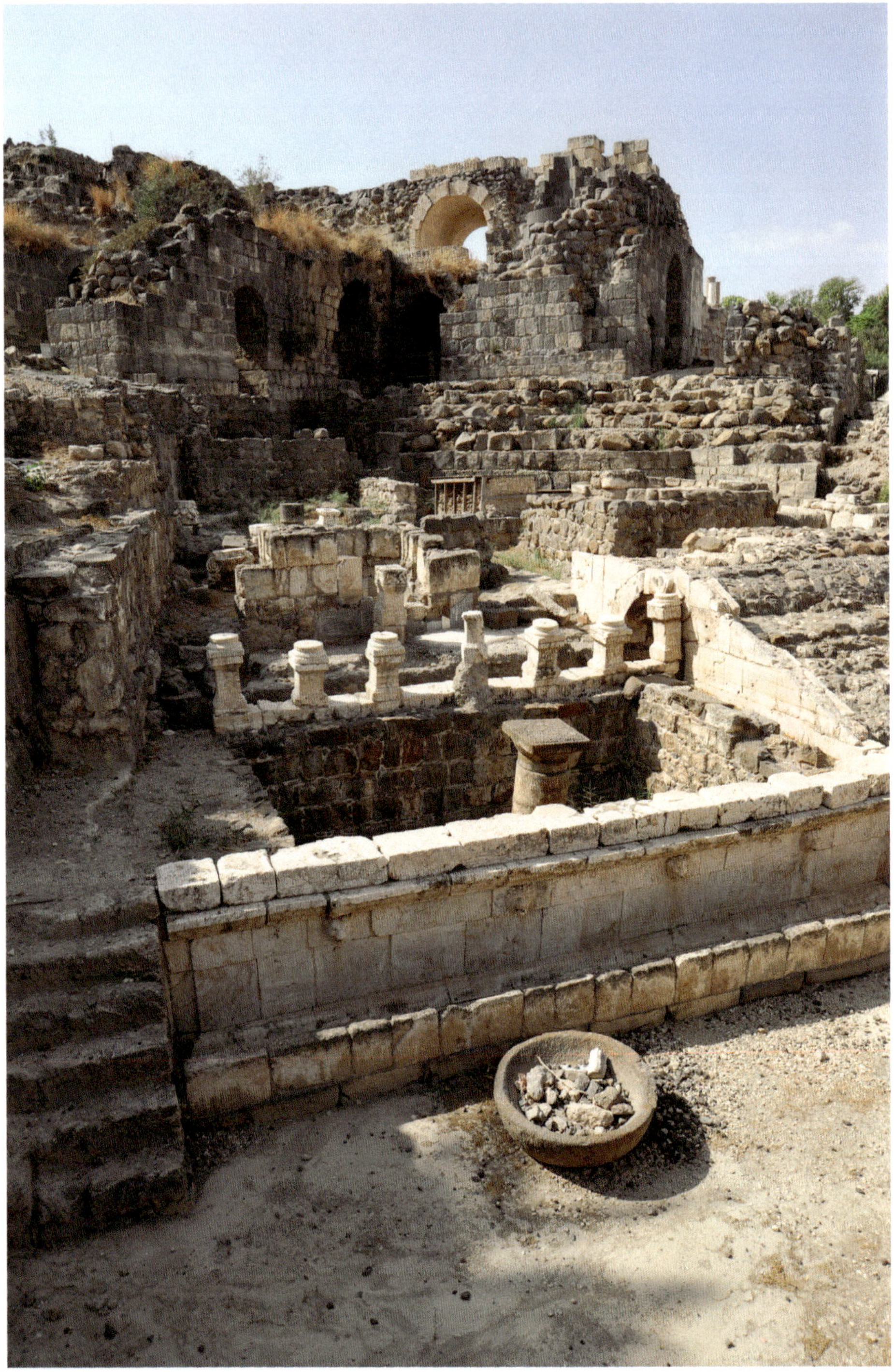

"So Saul died, and his three sons, and his armourbearer, and all his men, that same day together. And when the men of Israel that were on the other side of the valley, and they that were on the other side Jordan, saw that the men of Israel fled, and that Saul and his sons were dead, they forsook the cities, and fled; and the Philistines came and dwelt in them. And it came to pass on the morrow, when the Philistines came to strip the slain, that they found Saul and his three sons fallen in Mount Gilboa. And they cut off his head, and stripped off his armour, and sent into the land of the Philis-

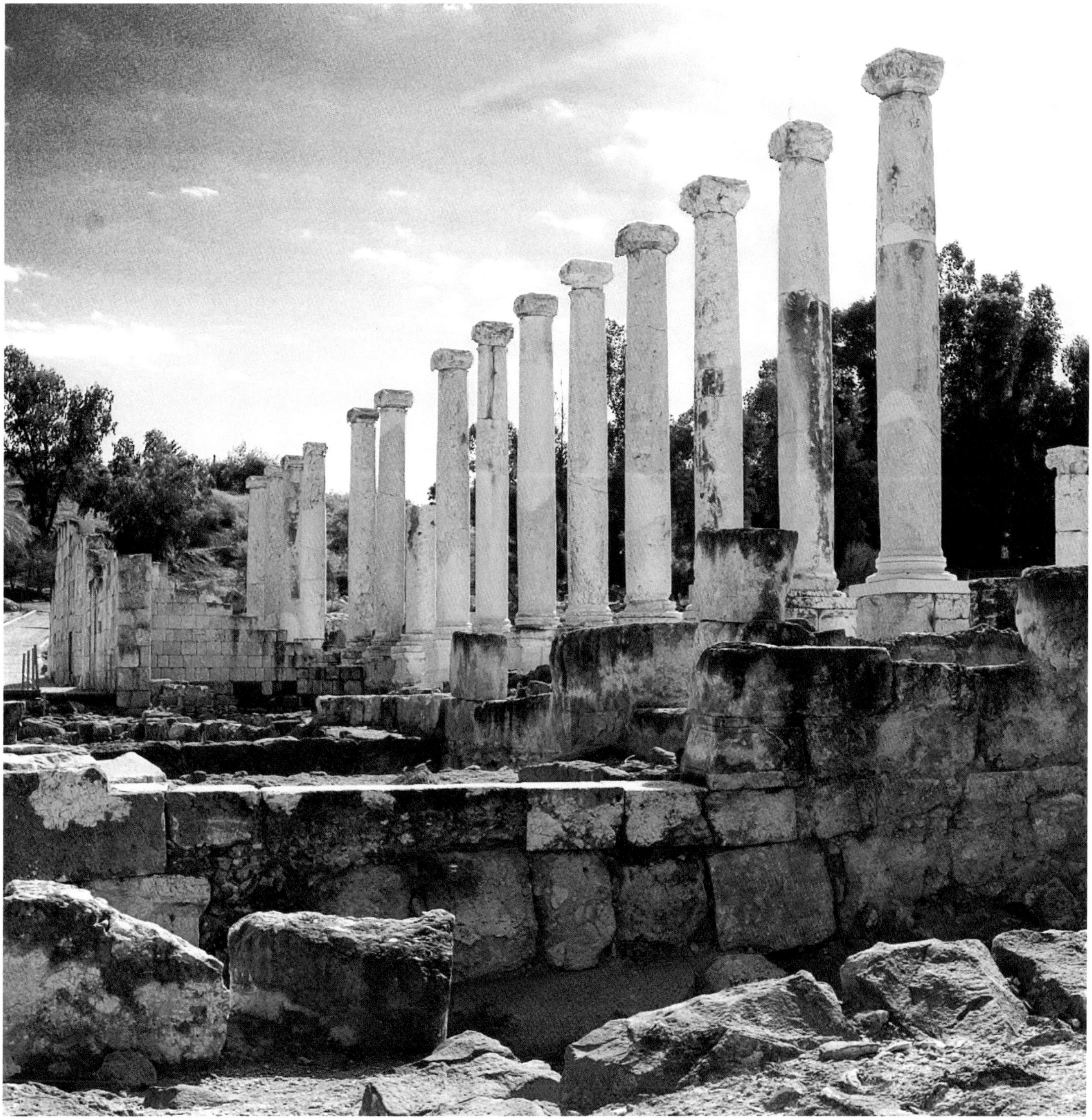

tines round about, to publish it in the house of their idols, and among the people. And they put his armour in the house of Ashtaroth: and they fastened his body to the wall of Bethshan [**Beit She'an**]. And when the inhabitants of Jabeshgilead heard of that which the Philistines had done to Saul; all the valiant men arose, and went all night, and took the body of Saul and the bodies of his sons from the wall of Bethshan, and came to Jabesh, and burnt them there. And they took their bones, and buried them under a tree at Jabesh, and fasted seven days."

– 1 Samuel 31:6-13 (KJV)

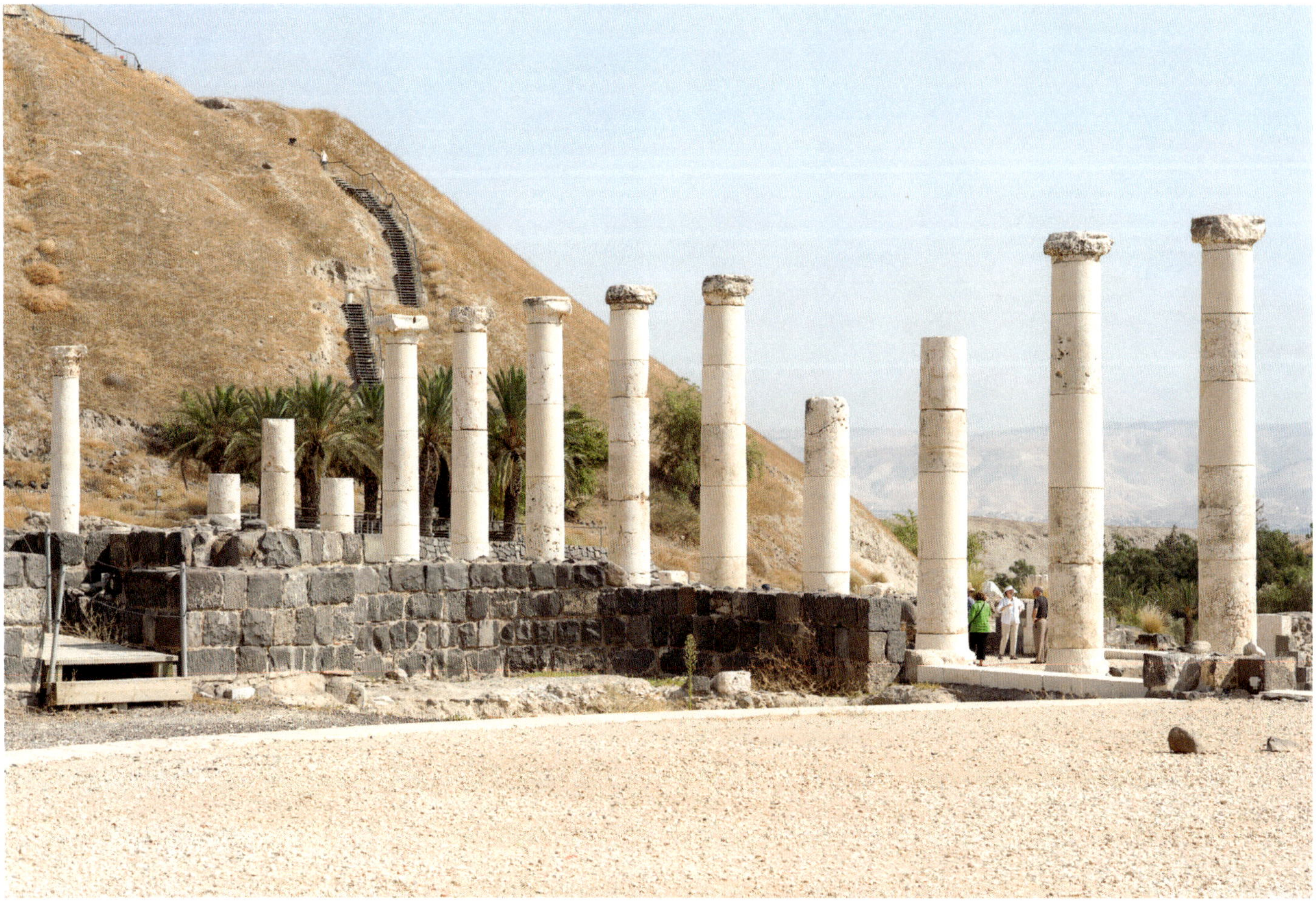

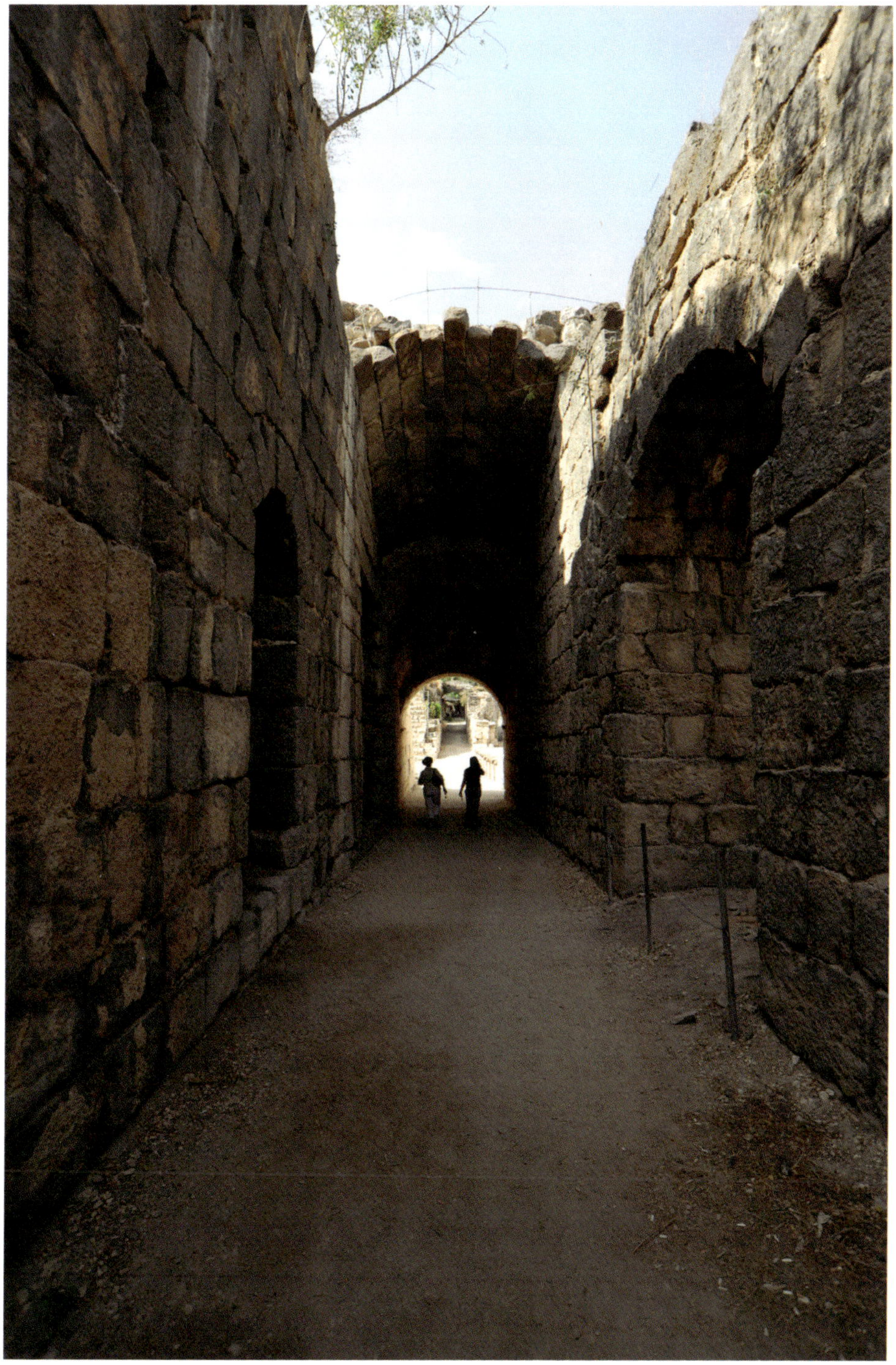

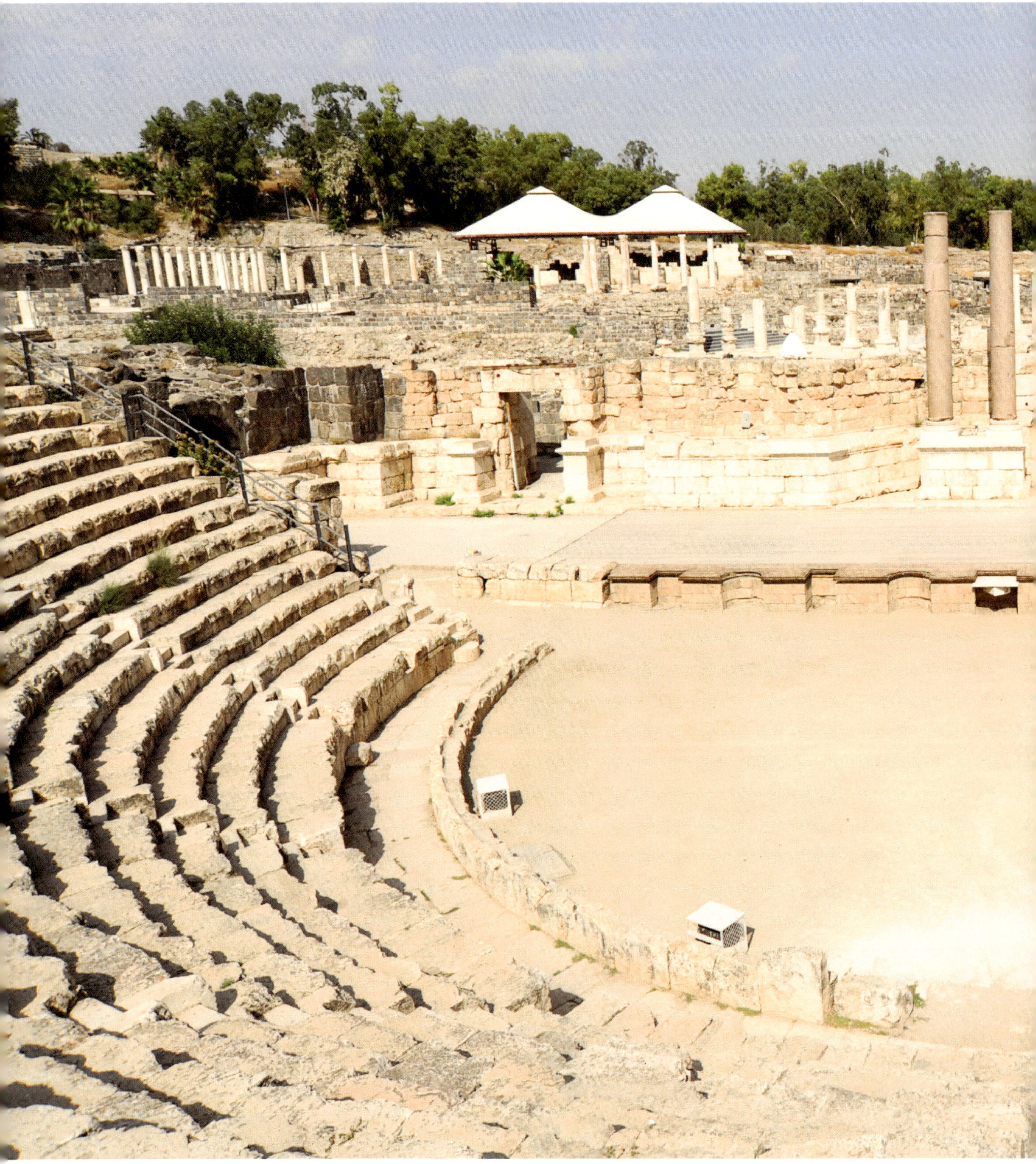

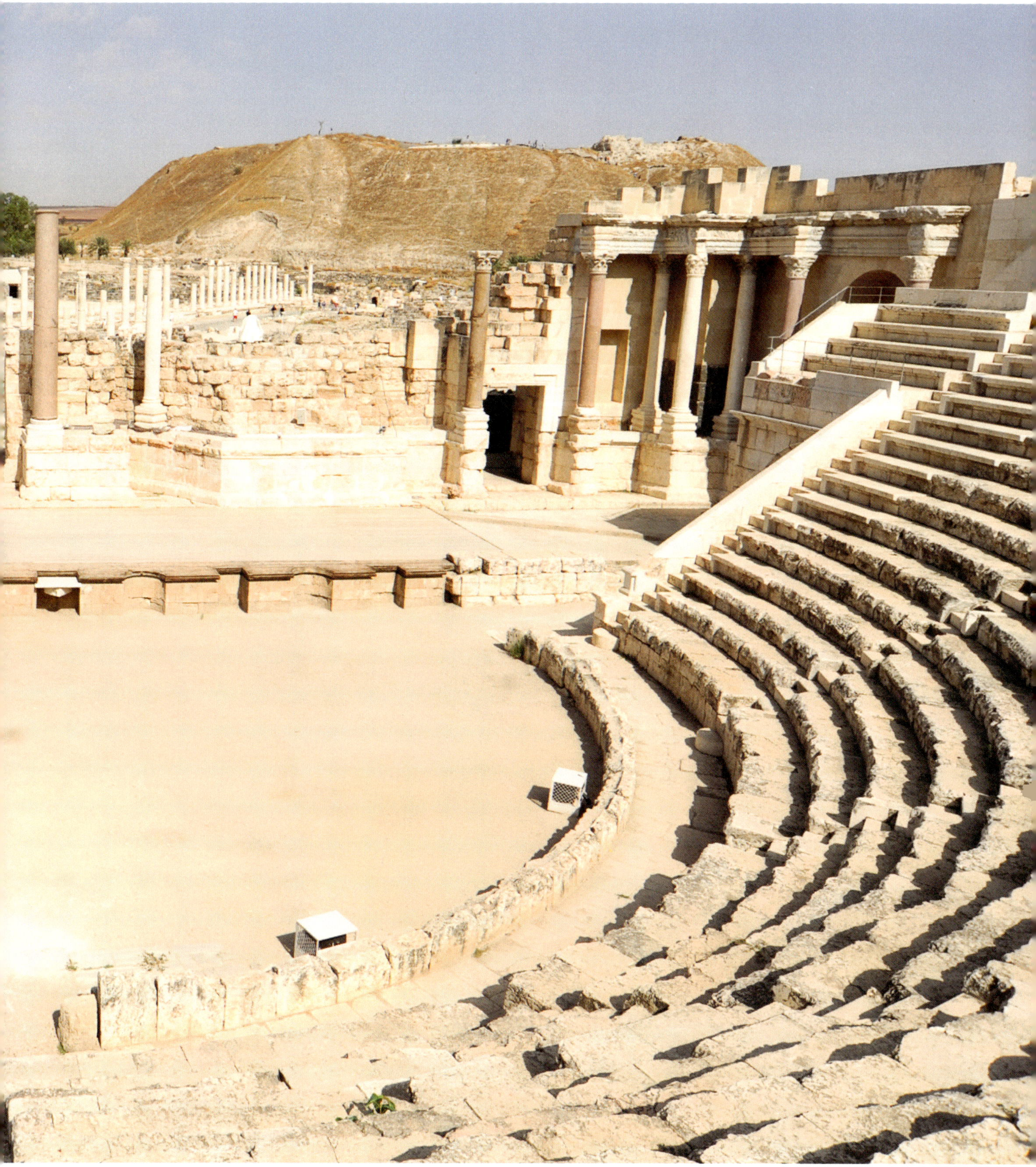

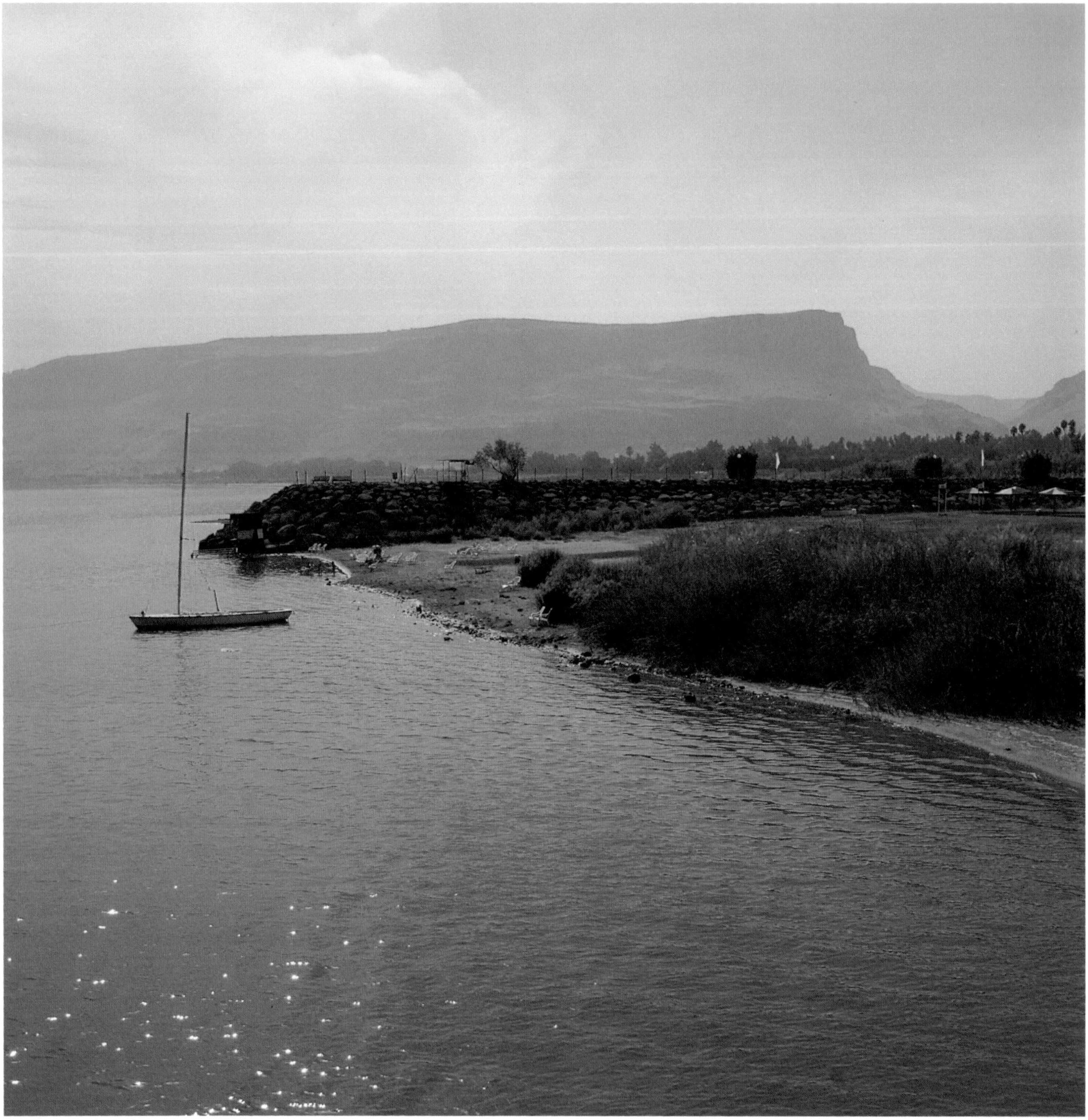

Pages 40-49: **Sea of Galilee and region**
The Sea of Galilee (or the Sea of Tiberias) is not actually a sea; it is a large freshwater lake at the headwaters of the Jordan River.

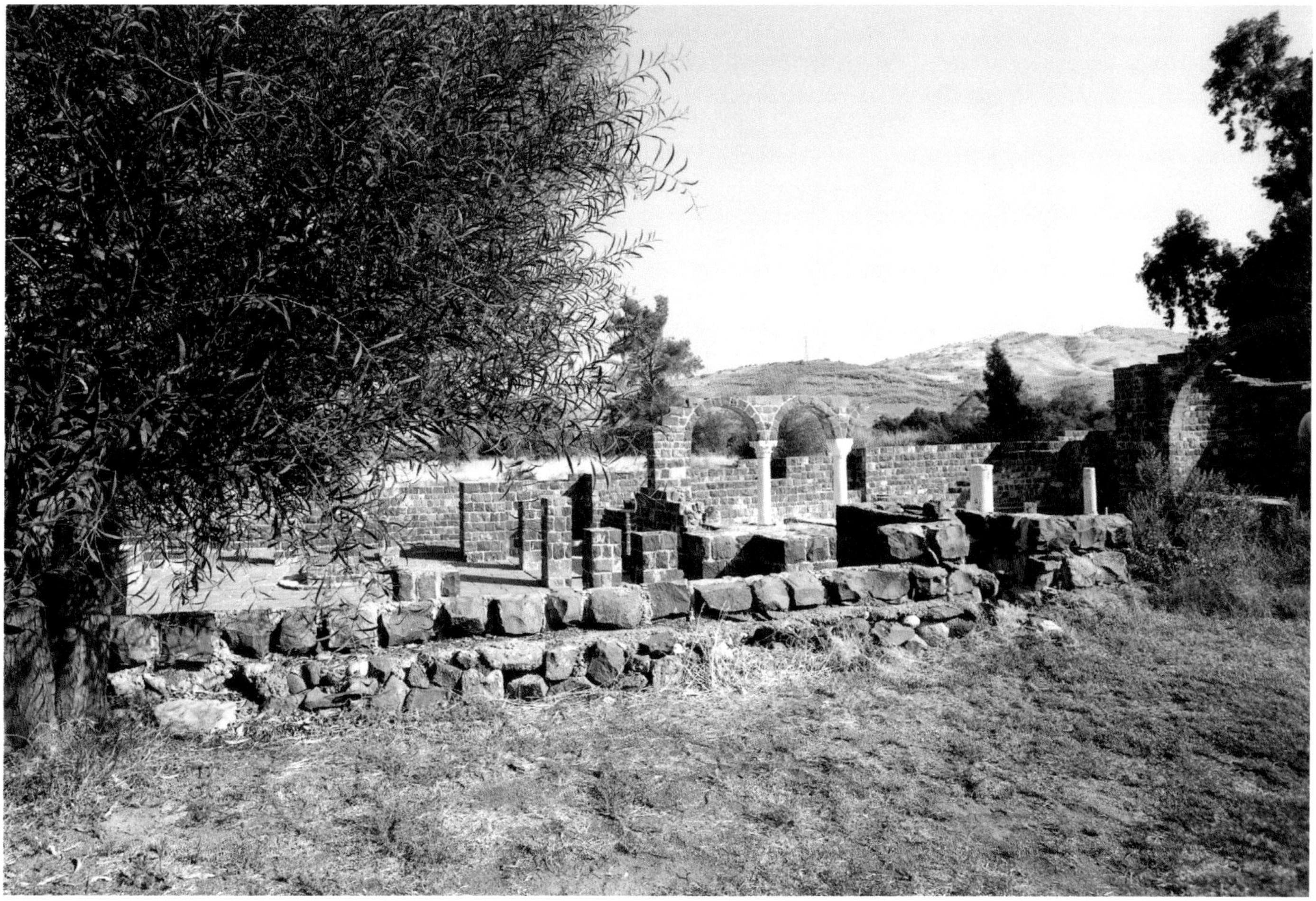

Above: **The far shore**
At the time of Jesus, the eastern shore of the sea was inhabited by non-Jews.

"They sailed to the region of the Gerasenes, which is across the lake from Galilee. When Jesus stepped ashore, He was met by a demon-possessed man from the town. [...] A large herd of pigs was feeding there on the hillside. The demons begged Jesus to let them go into them, and he gave them permission. When the demons came out of the man, they went into the pigs, and the herd rushed down the steep bank into the lake and was drowned. [...] Those who had seen it told the people how the demon-possessed man had been cured. Then all the people of the region of the Gerasenes asked Jesus to leave them, because they were overcome with fear. So He got into the boat and left. The man from whom the demons had gone out begged to go with Him, but Jesus sent him away, saying, 'Return home and tell how much God has done for you.' So the man went away and told all over town how much Jesus had done for him."

– Luke 8:26-27, 32-33, 36-39 (NIV)

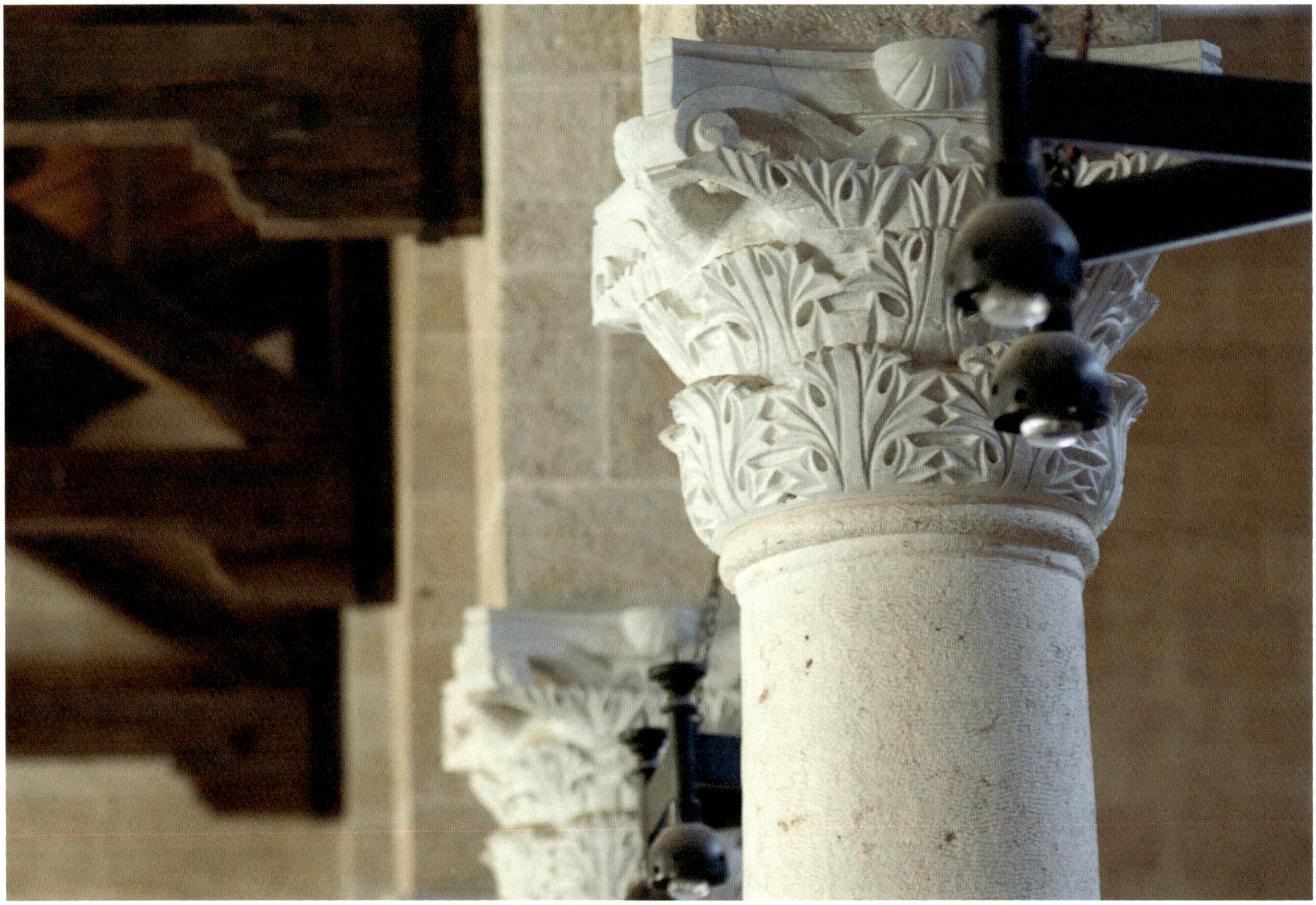

Above: **The Church of the Multiplication**
This church commemorates Jesus's feeding of the five thousand.

"After these things Jesus went over the sea of Galilee, which is the sea of Tiberias. And a great multitude followed Him, because they saw His miracles which He did on them that were diseased. And Jesus went up into a mountain, and there He sat with His disciples. And the passover, a feast of the Jews, was nigh. When Jesus then lifted up His eyes, and saw a great company come unto Him, He saith unto Philip, Whence shall we buy bread, that these may eat? And this He said to prove Him: for He Himself knew what He would do. Philip answered Him, Two hundred pennyworth of bread is not sufficient for them, that every one of them may take a little. One of His disciples, Andrew, Simon Peter's brother, saith unto Him, There is a lad here, which hath five barley loaves, and two small fishes: but what are they among so many? And Jesus said, Make the men sit down. Now there was much grass in the place. So the

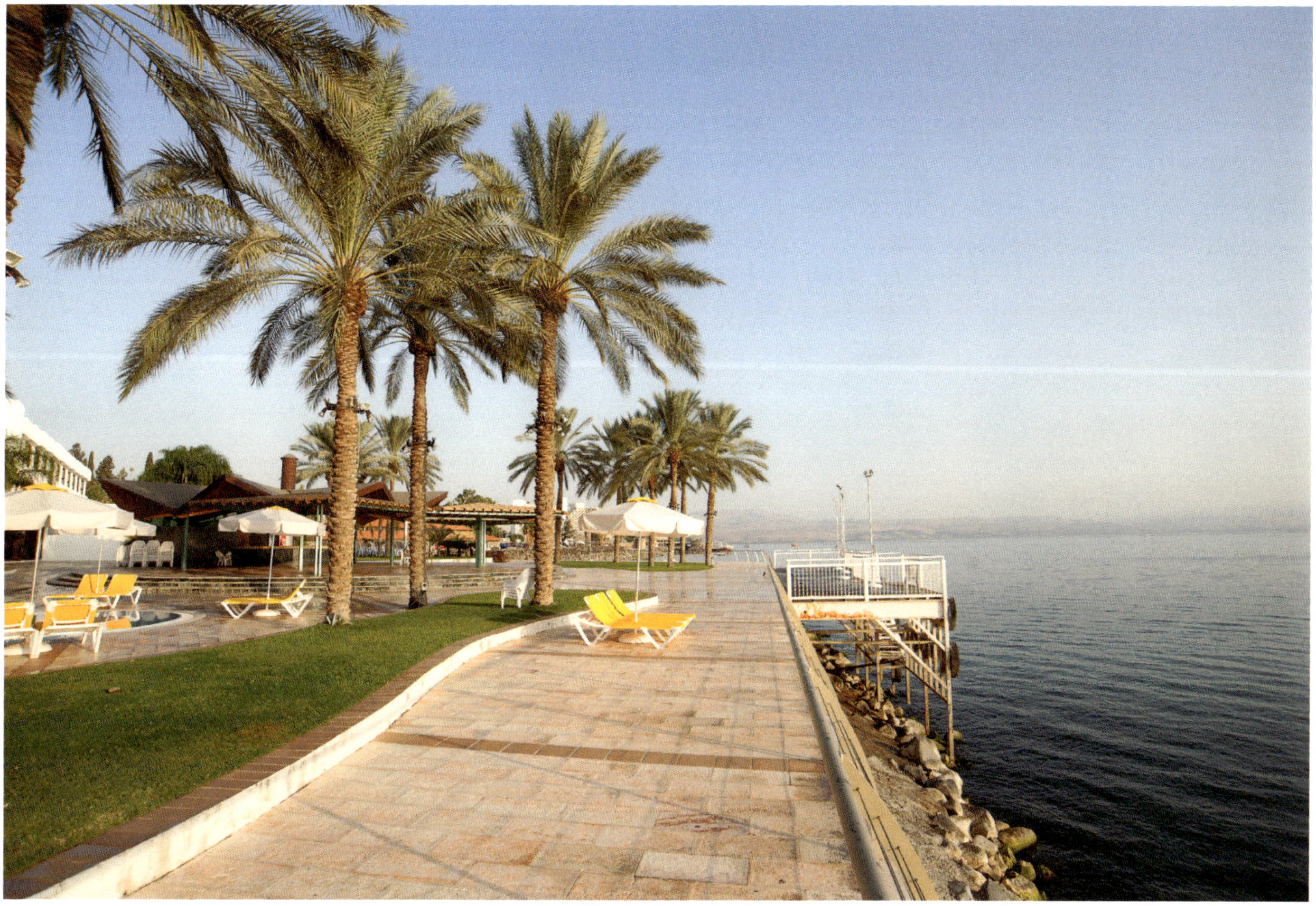

Above: **The town of Tiberias**
Tiberias became a center of Jewish culture and scholarship after the Roman expulsion of the Jews from Jerusalem in 135 A.D.

men sat down, in number about five thousand. And Jesus took the loaves; and when He had given thanks, He distributed to the disciples, and the disciples to them that were set down; and likewise of the fishes as much as they would. When they were filled, He said unto His disciples, Gather up the fragments that remain, that nothing be lost. Therefore they gathered them together, and filled twelve baskets with the fragments of the five barley loaves, which remained over and above unto them that had eaten. Then those men, when they had seen the miracle that Jesus did, said, This is of a truth that prophet that should come into the world. When Jesus therefore perceived that they would come and take Him by force, to make Him a king, He departed again into a mountain Himself alone."

– John 6:1-15 (KJV)

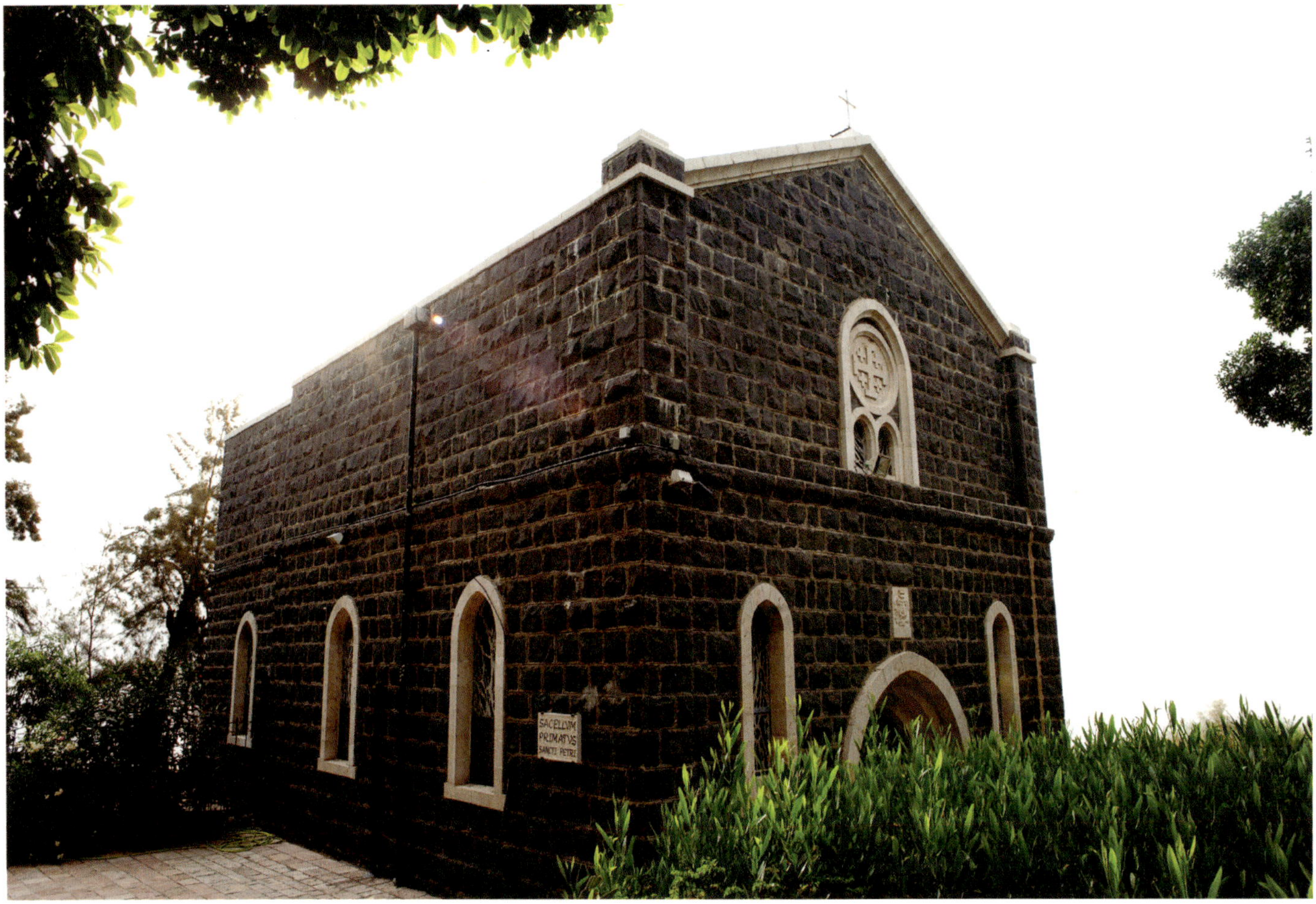

Pages 44 and 45: **The Church of the Primacy of St. Peter**

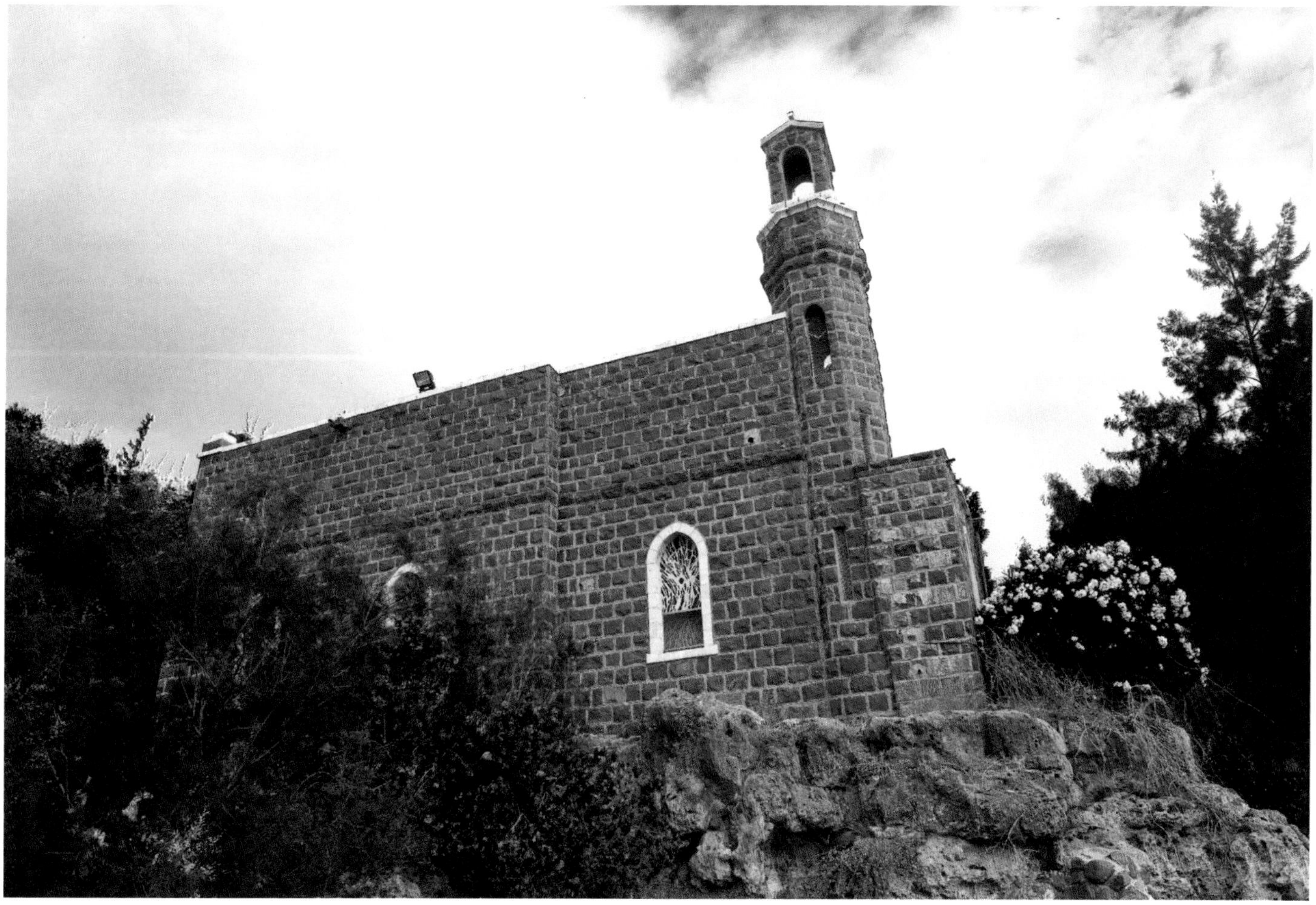

"Now when Jesus came into the district of Caesarea Philippi, He asked His disciples, 'Who do people say that the Son of Man is?' And they said, 'Some say John the Baptist, others say Elijah, and others Jeremiah or one of the prophets.' He said to them, 'But who do you say that I am?' Simon Peter replied, 'You are the Christ, the Son of the living God.' And Jesus answered him, 'Blessed are you, Simon Bar-Jonah! For flesh and blood has not revealed this to you, but my Father who is in heaven. And I tell you, you are Peter, and on this rock I will build my church, and the gates of hell shall not prevail against it.'"

– Matthew 16:13-18 (ESV)

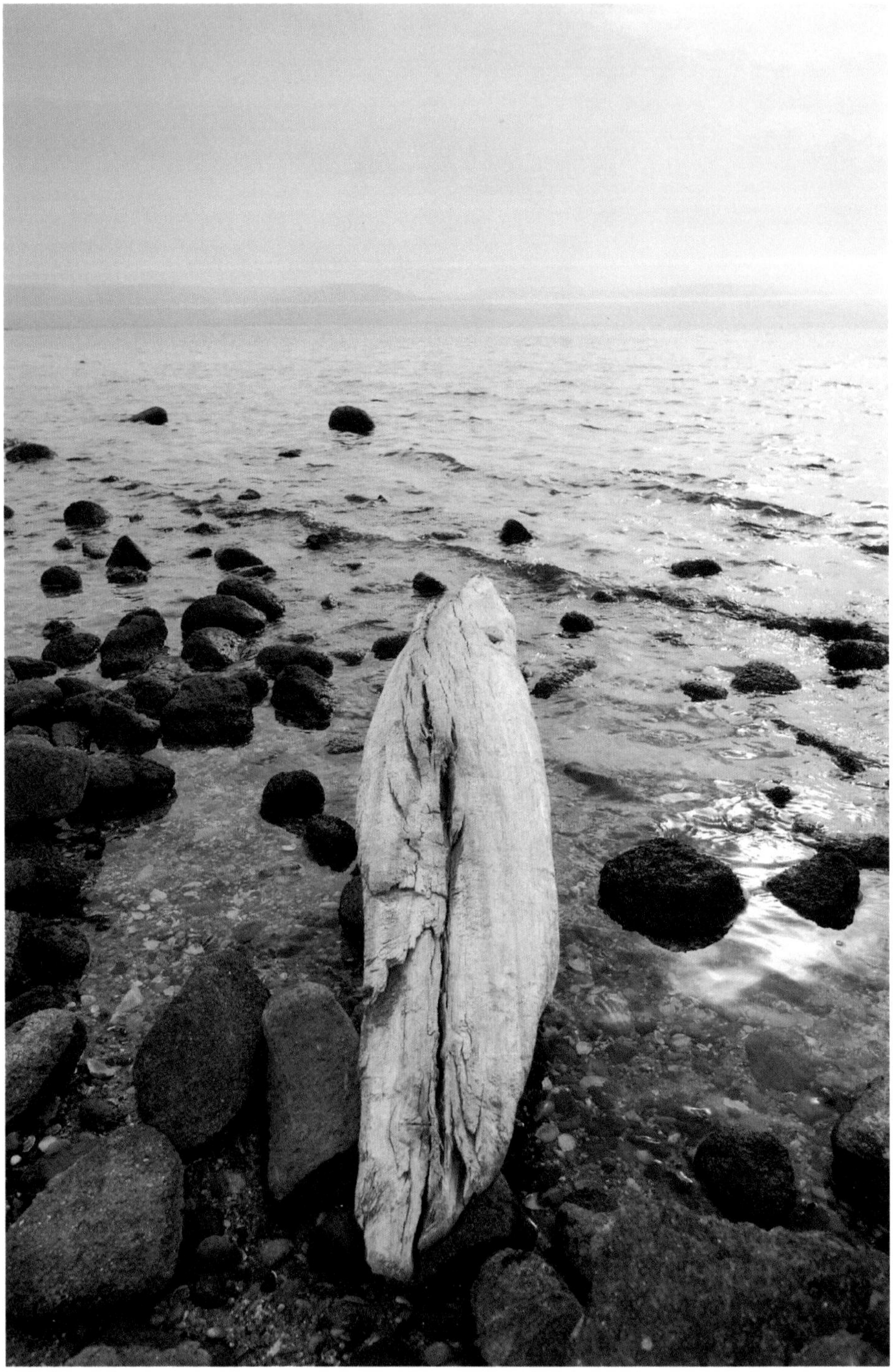

"Then He got into the boat and His disciples followed Him. Suddenly a furious storm came up on the lake, so that the waves swept over the boat. But Jesus was sleeping. The disciples went and woke Him, saying, 'Lord, save us! We're going to drown!' He replied, 'You of little faith, why are you so afraid?' Then He got up and rebuked the winds and the waves, and it was completely calm. The men were amazed and asked, 'What kind of man is this? Even the winds and the waves obey Him!'"

– Matthew 8:23-27 (NIV)

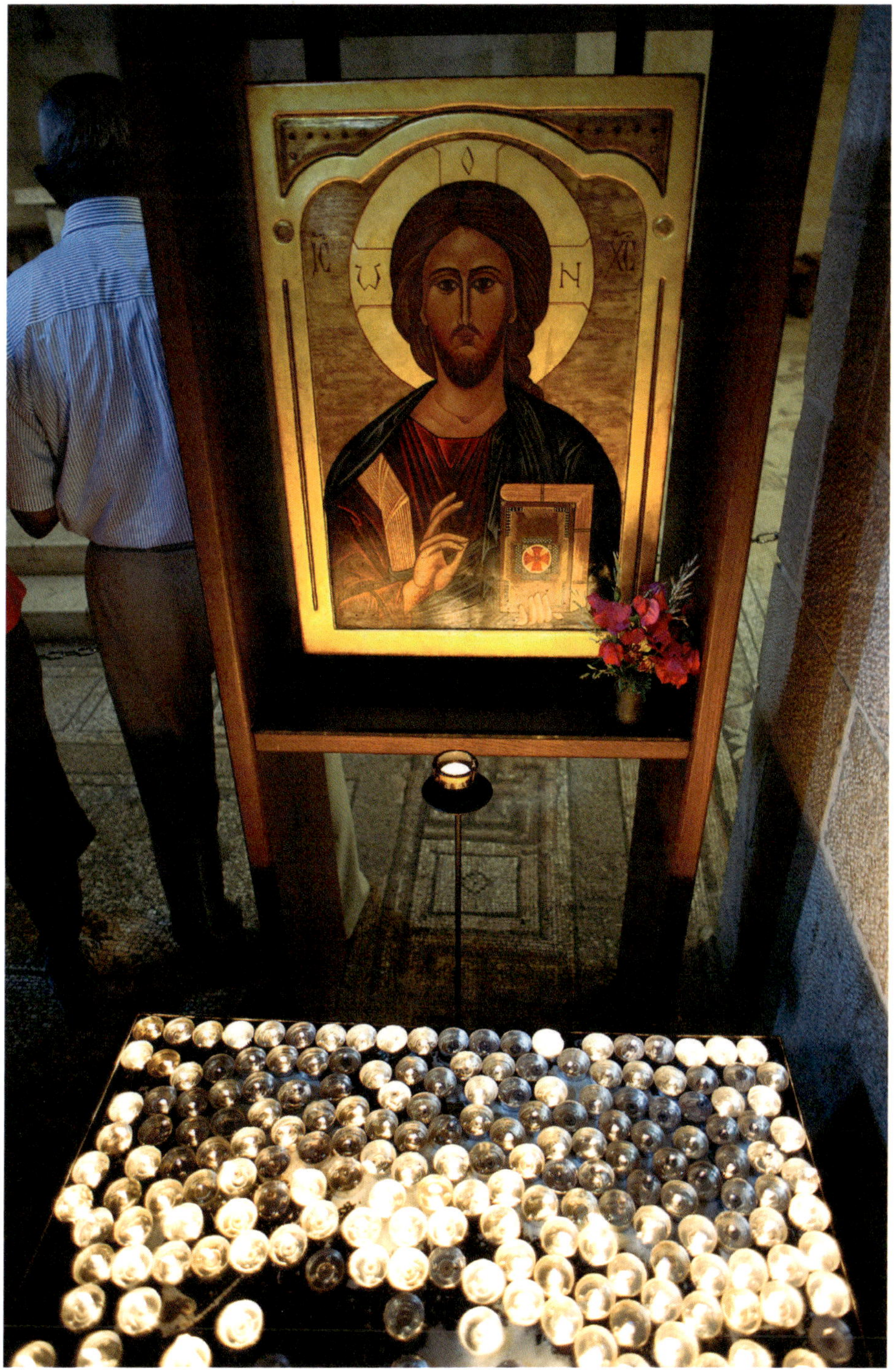

Left: **Sea of Galilee in fog**

Above: **Icon in the Church of the Multiplication**

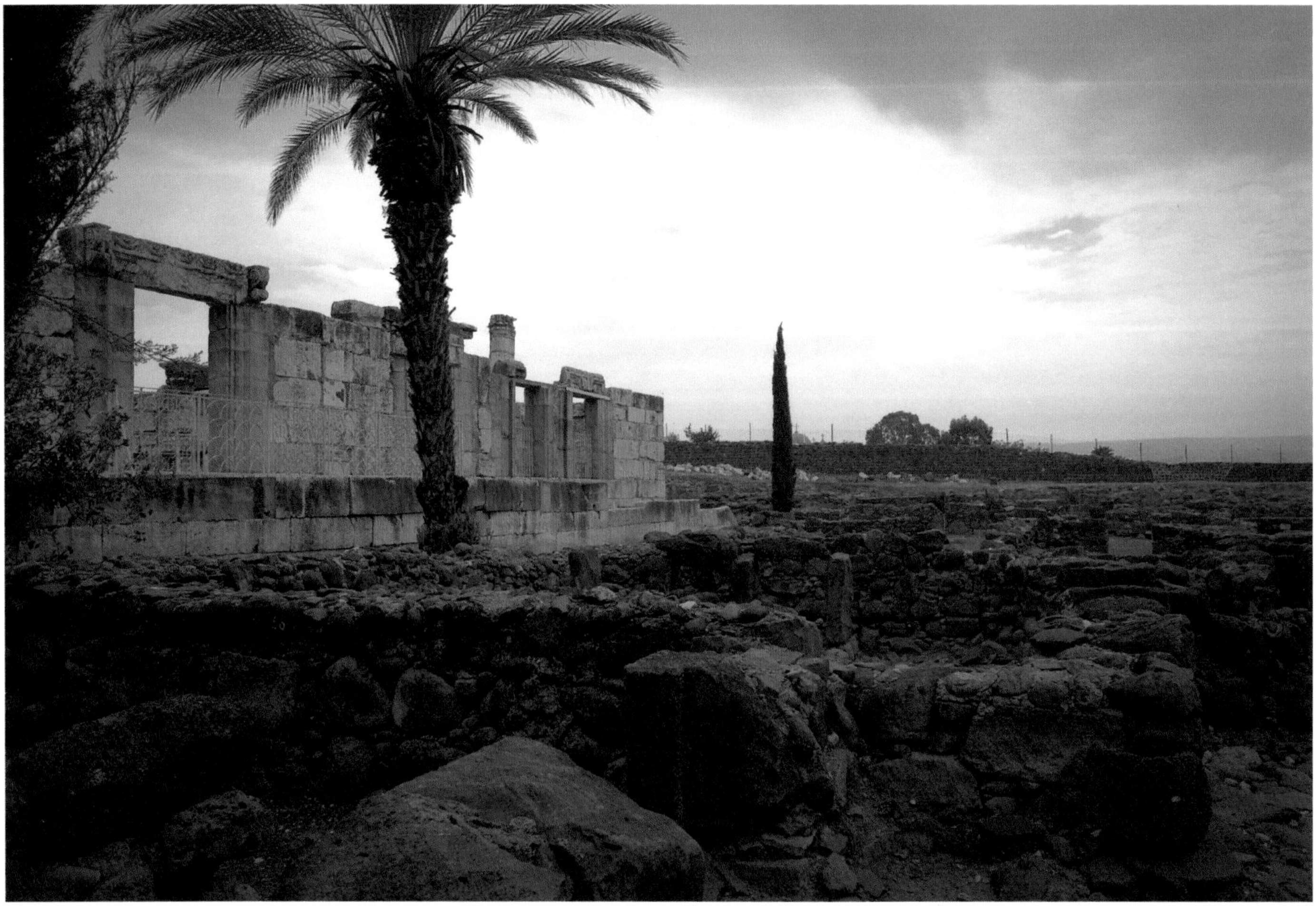

Above: **Capernaum**
Jesus lived and taught in this town next to the Sea of Galilee after leaving His childhood home of Nazareth.

"Then Jesus declared, 'I am the bread of life. He who comes to Me will never go hungry, and he who believes in Me will never be thirsty. But as I told you, you have seen Me and still you do not believe. All that the Father gives Me will come to Me, and whoever comes to Me I will never drive away. For I have come down from heaven not to do My will but to do the will of Him who sent Me. And this is the will of Him who sent Me, that I shall lose none of all that He has given Me, but raise them up at the last day. For my Father's will is that everyone who looks to the Son and believes in Him shall have eternal life, and I will raise them up at the last day.' [...] Jesus said to them, 'Very truly I tell you, unless you eat the flesh

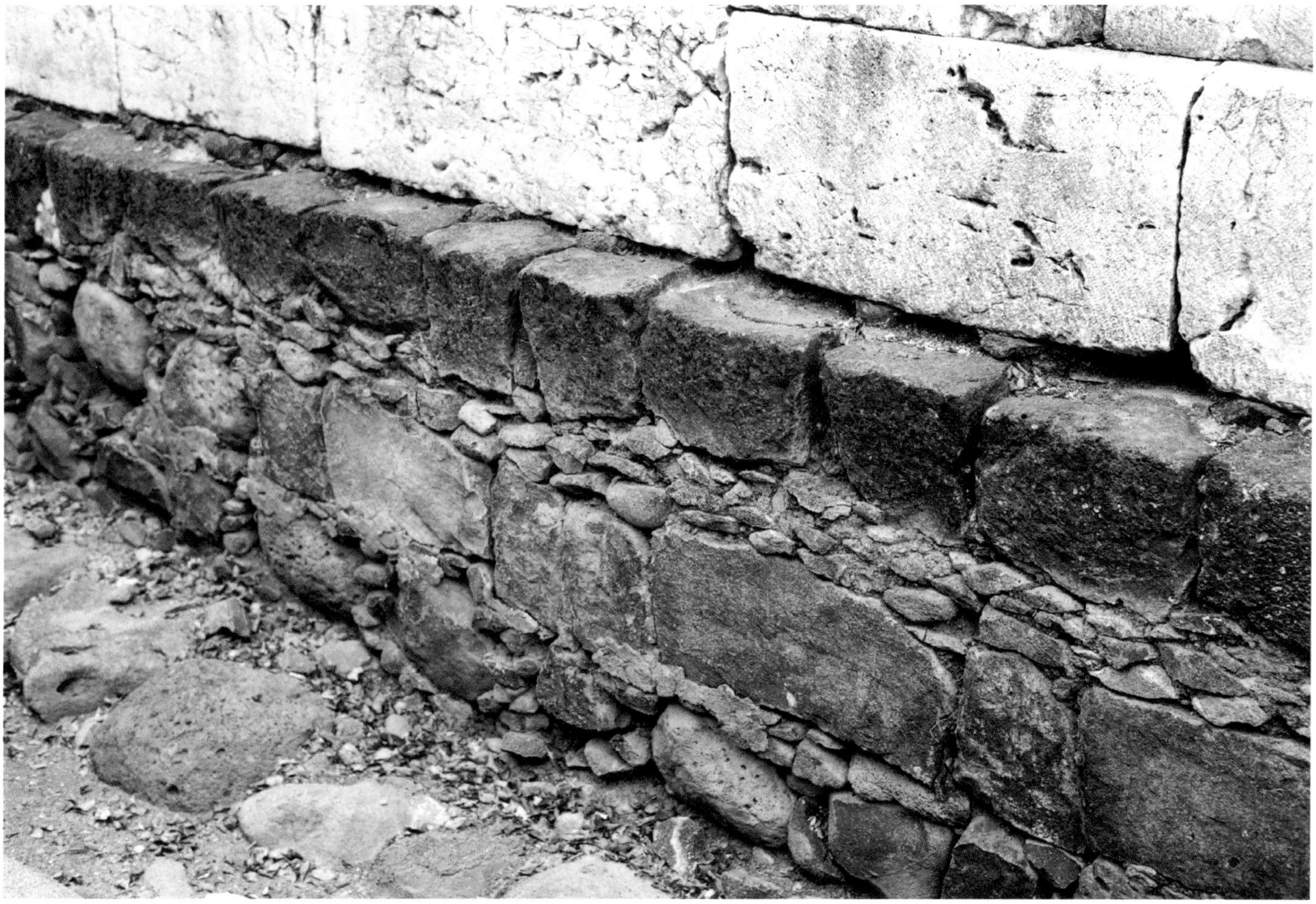

Above: **The Capernaum synagogue**
The lower, dark layer dates from the time of Jesus.

of the Son of Man and drink His blood, you have no life in you. Whoever eats My flesh and drinks My blood has eternal life, and I will raise them up at the last day. For My flesh is real food and My blood is real drink. Whoever eats My flesh and drinks My blood remains in Me, and I in Him. Just as the living Father sent me and I live because of the Father, so the one who feeds on Me will live because of Me. This is the bread that came down from heaven. Your ancestors ate manna and died, but whoever feeds on this bread will live forever.' He said this while teaching in the synagogue in Capernaum."

– John 6:35-40, 53-59 (NIV)

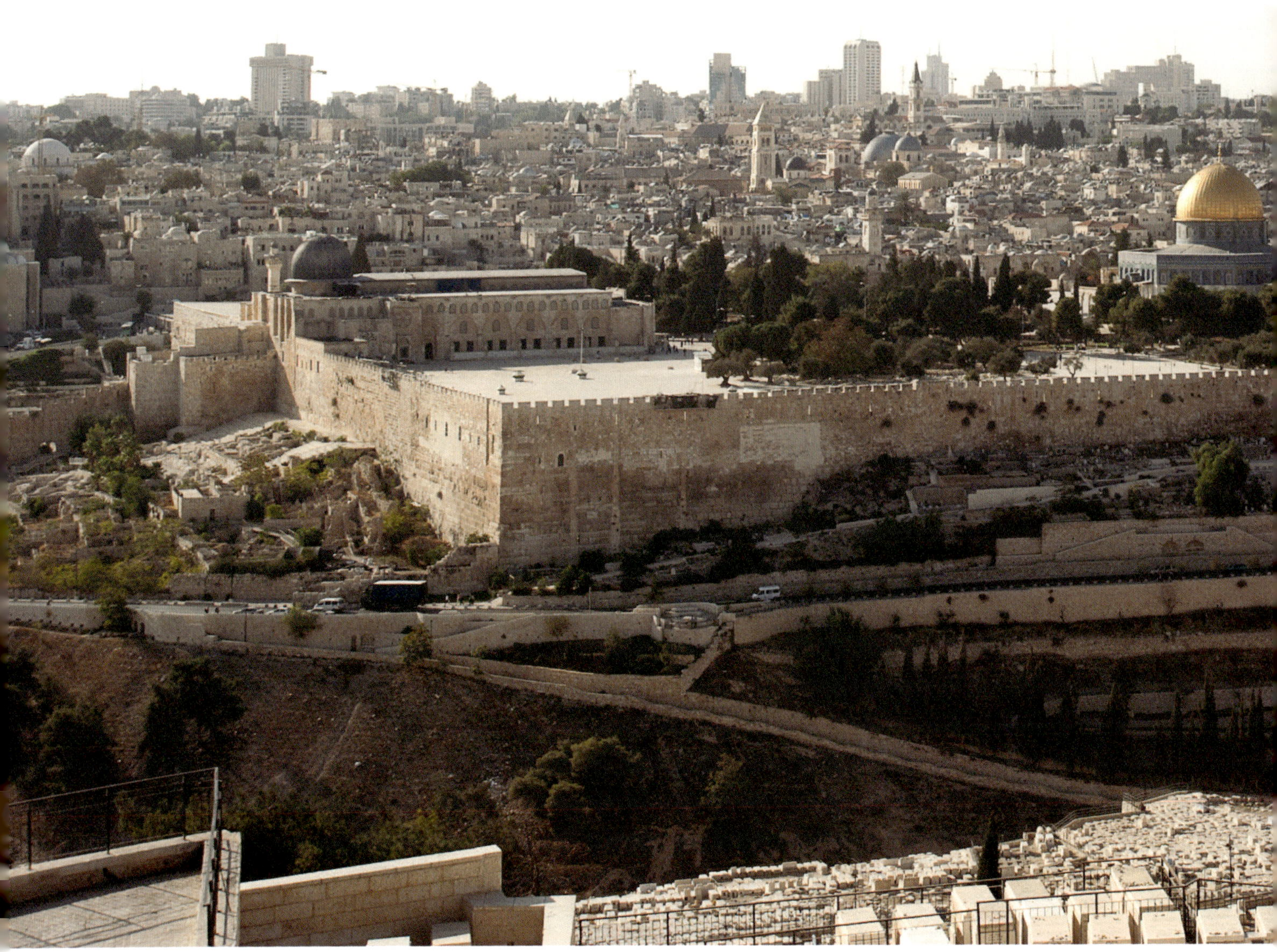

Above: **The Temple Mount and Jerusalem viewed from the Mount of Olives**
This is the site of Ornan's threshing floor, purchased by David in 1 Chronicles 21, where Solomon's Temple was later built. The first temple was destroyed by the Babylonians around 590 B.C. Zerubbabel rebuilt the temple some 70 years later. It stood atop this stone platform until its destruction in 70 A.D. The gold structure is the Dome of the Rock, one of the two Islamic sites built on the platform between 689 and 1035. Along with the Al-Aqsa Mosque (the black dome to the left), it is part of the third holiest site in Islam.

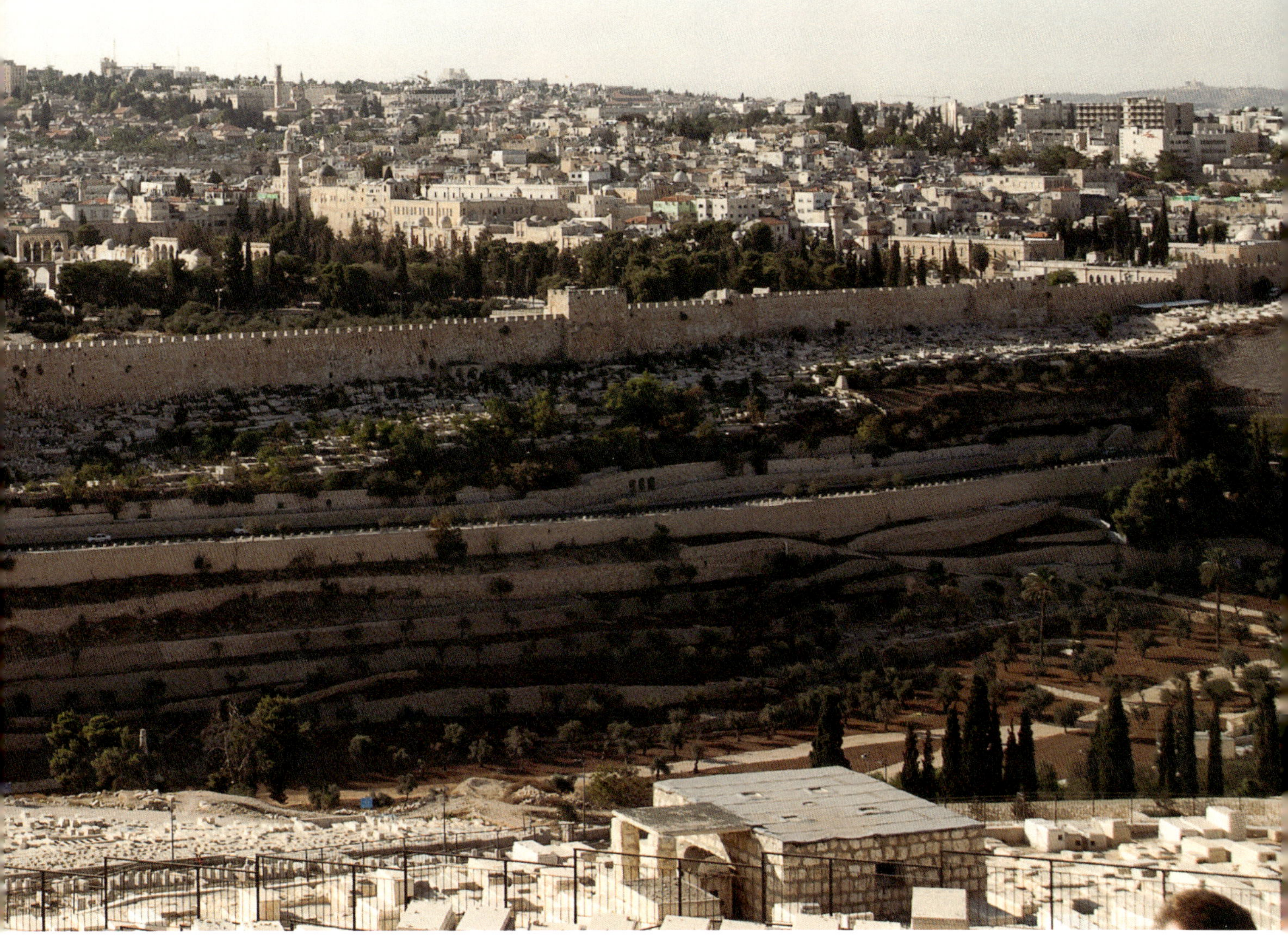

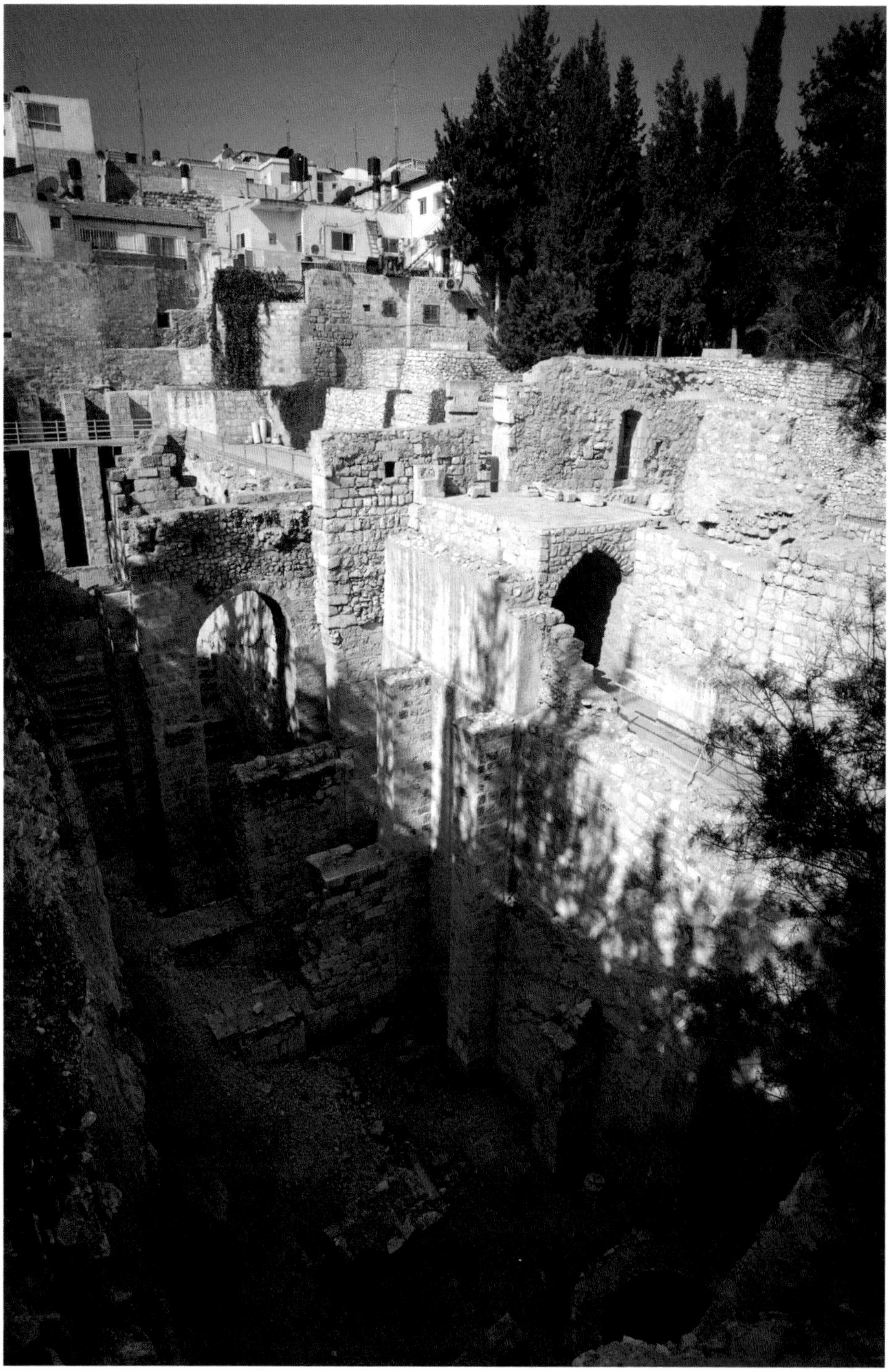

"After this there was a feast of the Jews, and Jesus went up to Jerusalem. Now there is in Jerusalem by the Sheep Gate a pool, in Aramaic called Bethesda, which has five roofed colonnades. In these lay a multitude of invalids – blind, lame, and paralyzed. One man was there who had been an invalid for thirty-eight years. When Jesus saw him lying there and knew that he had already been there a long time, He said to him, 'Do you want to be healed?' The sick man answered Him, 'Sir, I have no one to put me into the pool when the water is stirred up, and while I am going another steps down before me.' Jesus said to him, 'Get up, take up your bed, and walk.' And at once the man was healed, and he took up his bed and walked. Now that day was the Sabbath. So the Jews said to the man who had been healed, 'It is the Sabbath, and it is not lawful for you to take up your bed.' But he answered them, 'The man who healed me, that man said to me, 'Take up your bed, and walk."' They asked him, 'Who is the man

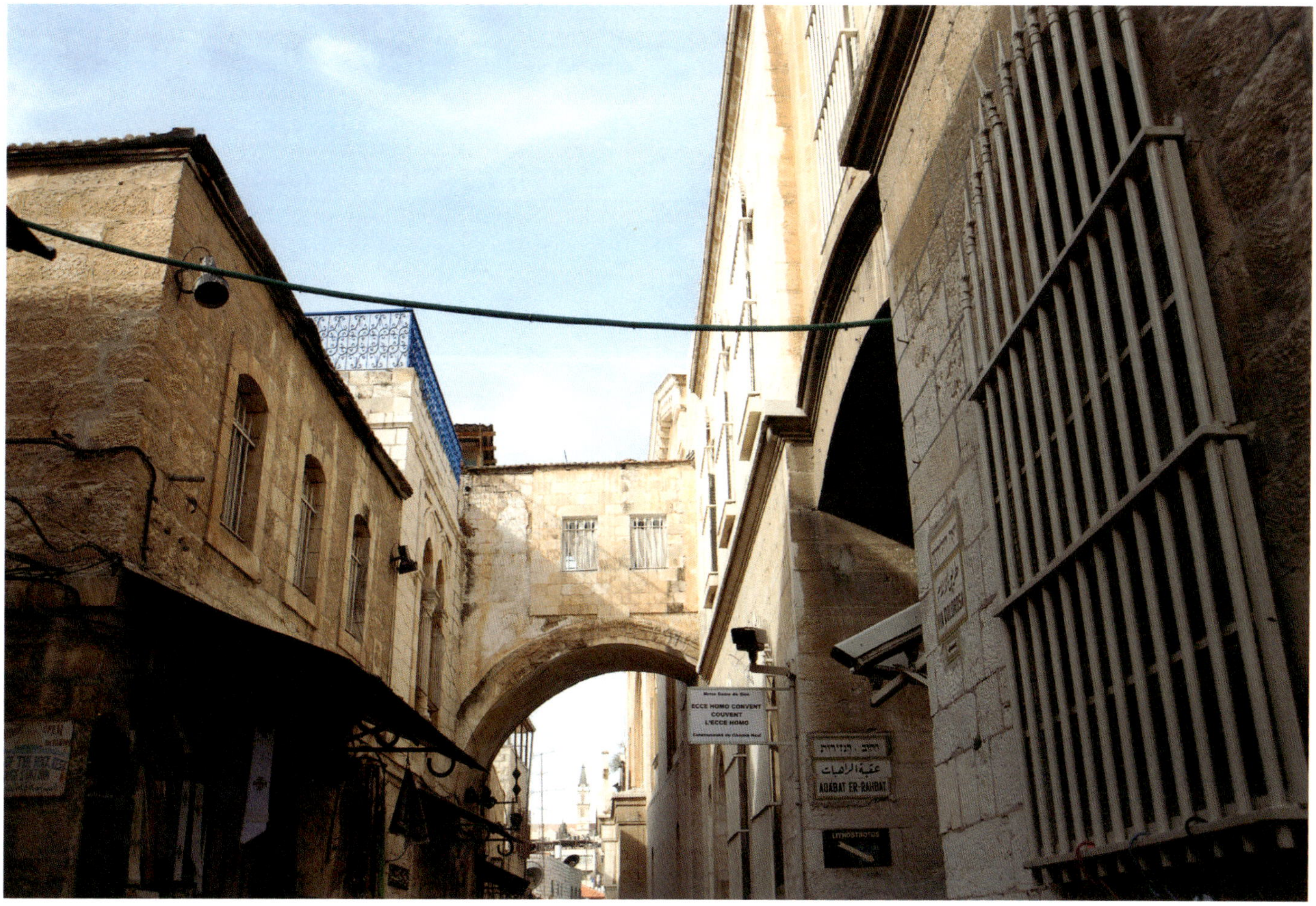

Left: **Pool of Bethesda**

Pages 50-61: **Jerusalem**

Jerusalem has been destroyed many times. Each time, the inhabitants have smoothed out the rubble and built on top of it. As a result, the city is striated, with older material found deeper. In some places, remains from Jesus's day are located thirty feet below modern street level.

who said to you, 'Take up your bed and walk'?" Now the man who had been healed did not know who it was, for Jesus had withdrawn, as there was a crowd in the place. Afterward Jesus found him in the temple and said to him, 'See, you are well! Sin no more, that nothing worse may happen to you.' The man went away and told the Jews that it was Jesus who had healed him. And this was why the Jews were persecuting Jesus, because He was doing these things on the Sabbath. But Jesus answered them, 'My Father is working until now, and I am working.' This was why the Jews were seeking all the more to kill Him, because not only was He breaking the Sabbath, but He was even calling God his own Father, making Himself equal with God."

– John 5:1-18 (ESV)

Below: **Muslim Quarter of the Old City of Jerusalem**

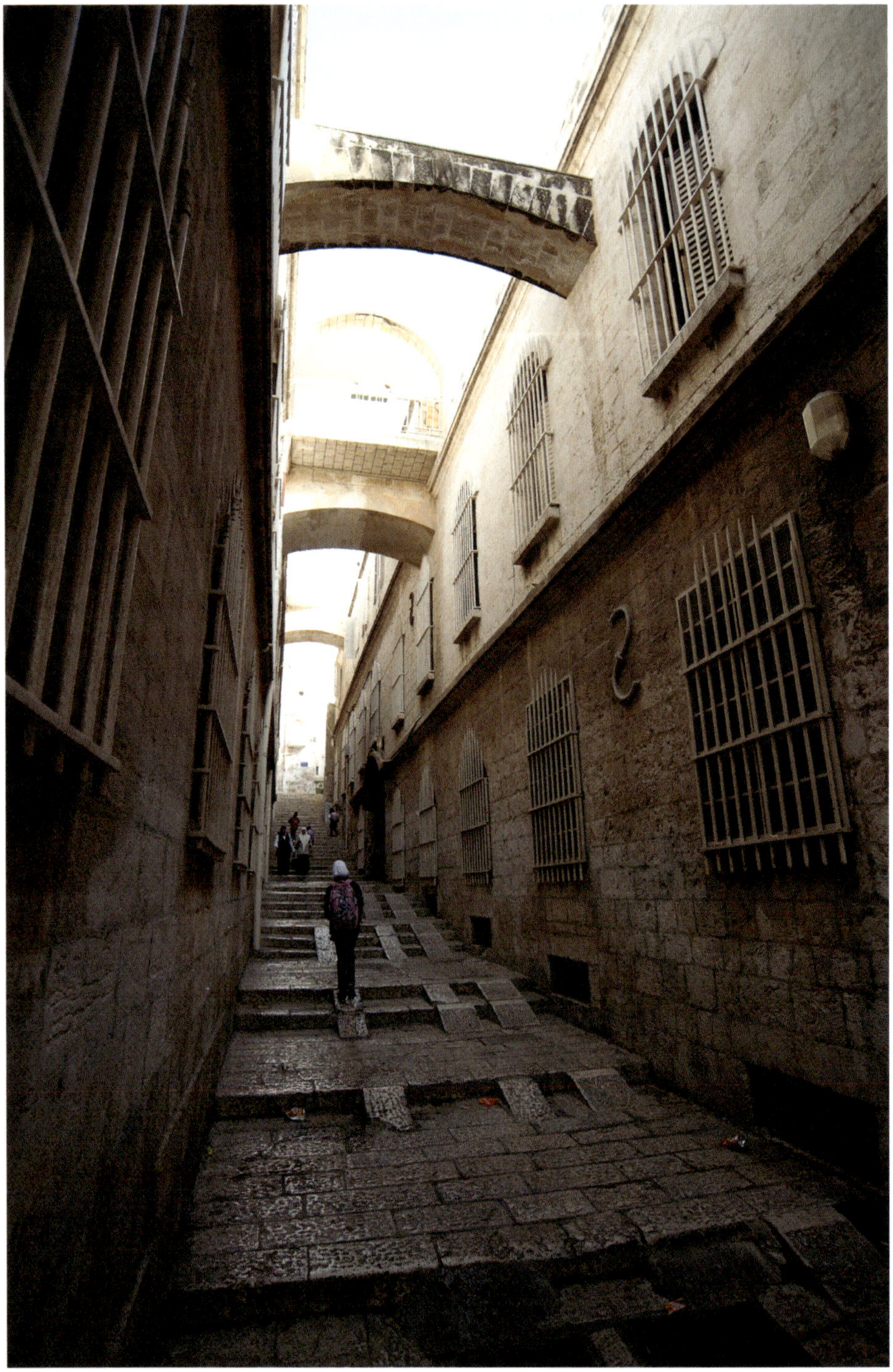

"Jesus said to them, 'If God were your Father, you would love Me, for I came from God and I am here. I came not of My own accord, but He sent Me. Why do you not understand what I say? It is because you cannot bear to hear My word. You are of your father the devil, and your will is to do your father's desires. He was a murderer from the beginning, and has nothing to do with the truth, because there is no truth in him. When he lies, he speaks out of his own character, for he is a liar and the father of lies. But because I tell the truth, you do not believe Me. Which one of you convicts Me of sin? If I tell the truth, why do you not believe Me? Whoever is of God hears the words of God. The reason why you do not hear them is that you are not of God.' The Jews answered Him, 'Are we not right in saying that You are a Samaritan and have a demon?' Jesus answered, 'I do not have a demon, but I honor my Father, and you dishonor Me. Yet I do not seek My own glory; there is One who seeks it, and He is the judge. Truly, truly, I say to you, if anyone keeps My word, he will never see death.' The Jews said to Him, 'Now we know that

Below: **The Southern Wall of the Temple Mount**

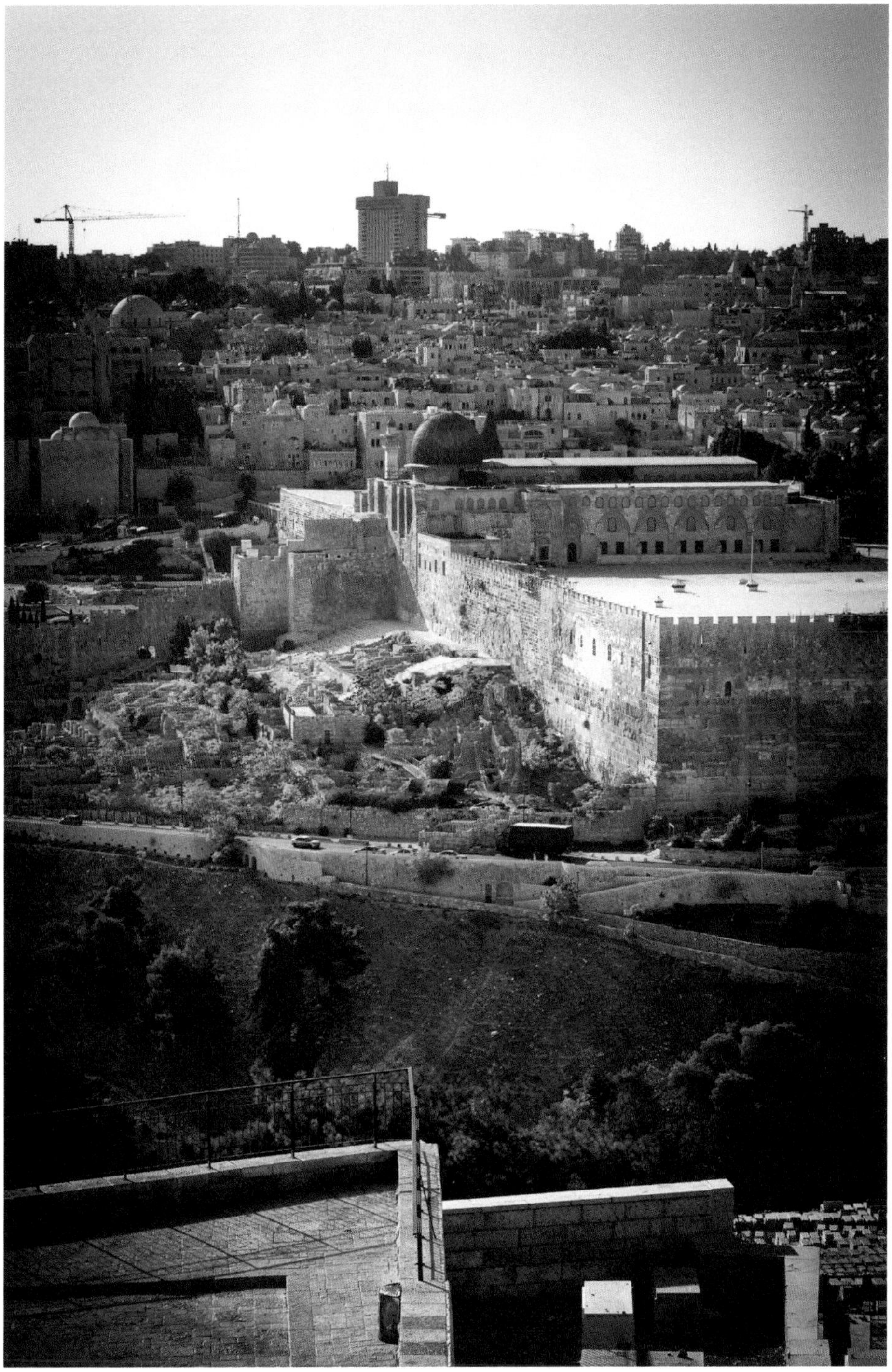

You have a demon! Abraham died, as did the prophets, yet You say, 'If anyone keeps My word, he will never taste death.' Are You greater than our father Abraham, who died? And the prophets died! Who do You make yourself out to be?' Jesus answered, 'If I glorify Myself, My glory is nothing. It is My Father who glorifies Me, of whom you say, 'He is our God.' But you have not known Him. I know Him. If I were to say that I do not know Him, I would be a liar like you, but I do know Him and I keep His word. Your father Abraham rejoiced that he would see My day. He saw it and was glad.' So the Jews said to Him, 'You are not yet fifty years old, and have You seen Abraham?' Jesus said to them, 'Truly, truly, I say to you, before Abraham was, I am.' So they picked up stones to throw at Him, but Jesus hid Himself and went out of the temple."

– John 8:42-59 (ESV)

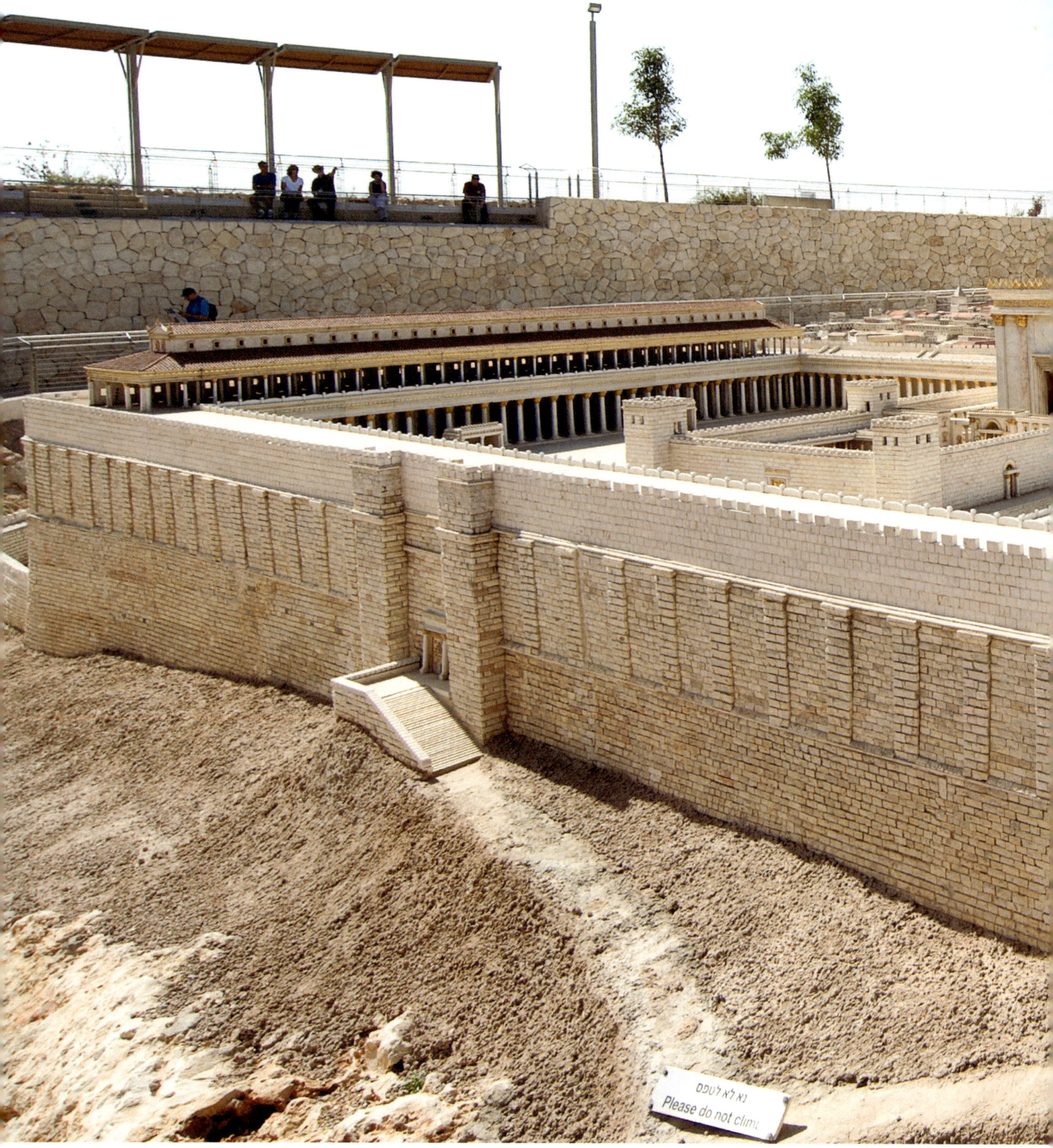
נא לא לטפס
Please do not clim

1:50 scale model of Second Jewish Temple and complex circa 70 A.D., Israel Museum

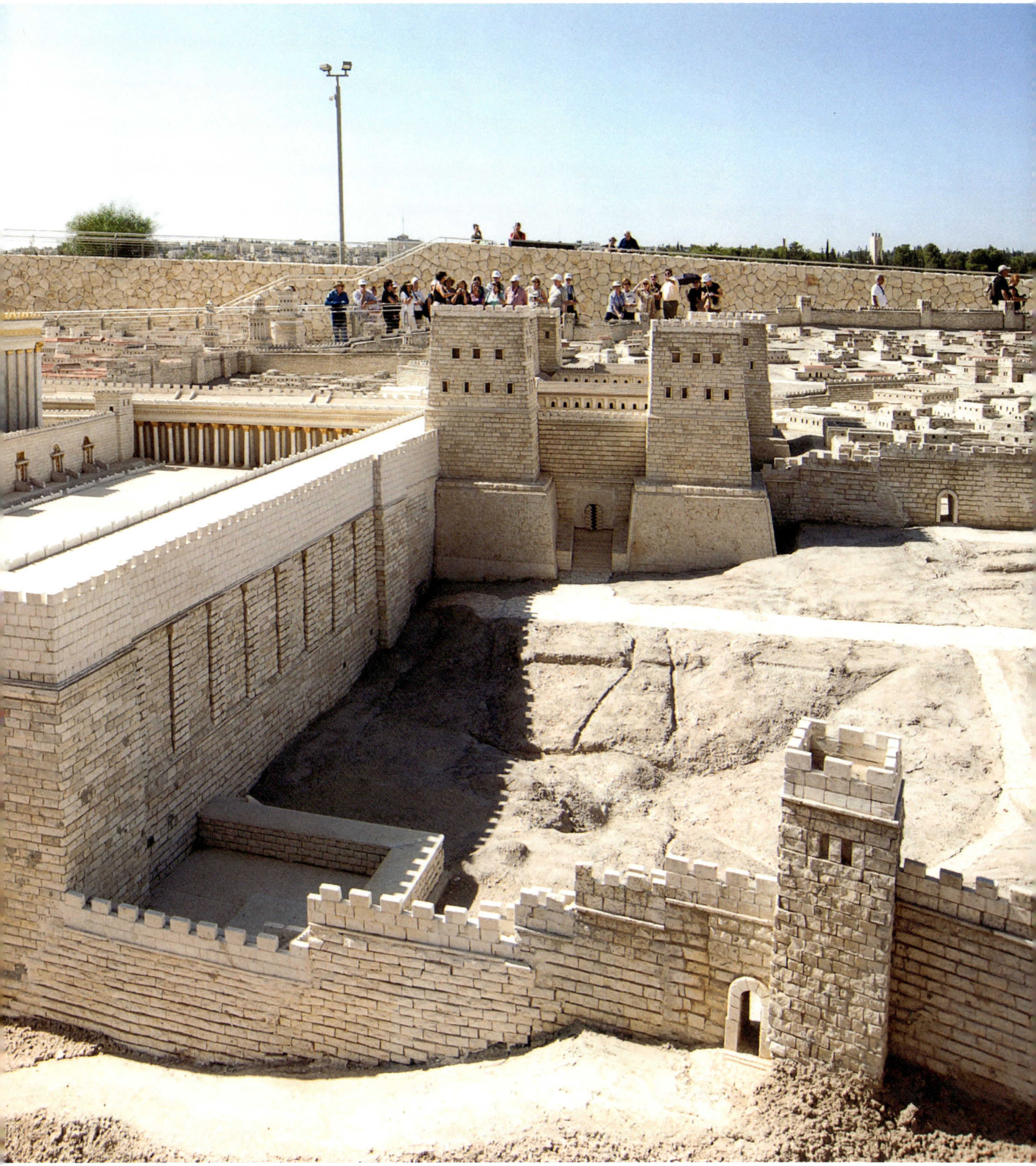

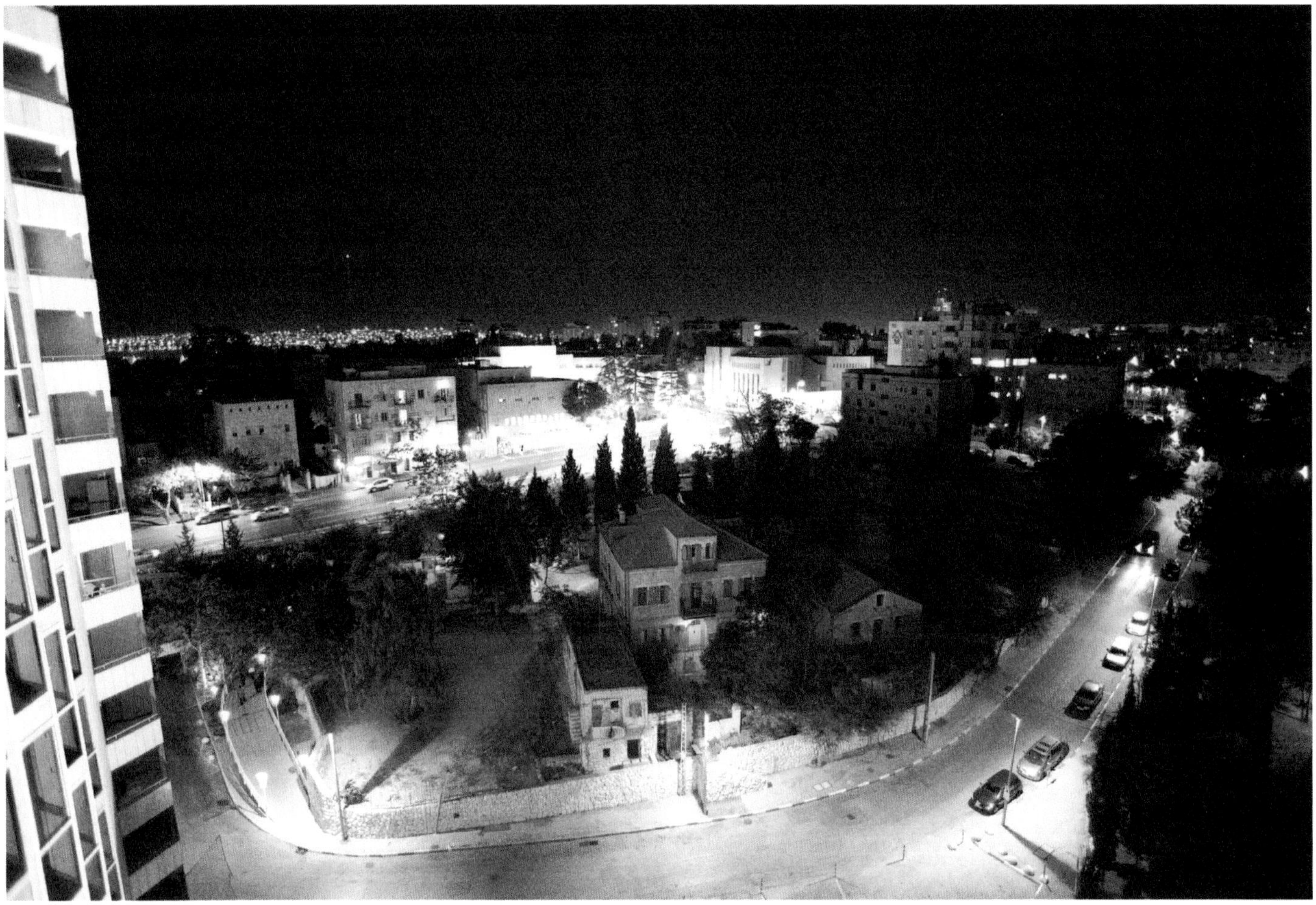

Above: **Jerusalem at night**

"You are the light of the world. A city set on a hill cannot be hidden. Nor do people light a lamp and put it under a basket, but on a stand, and it gives light to all in the house. In the same way, let your light shine before others, so that they may see your good works and give glory to your Father who is in heaven."

– Matthew 5:14-16 (ESV)

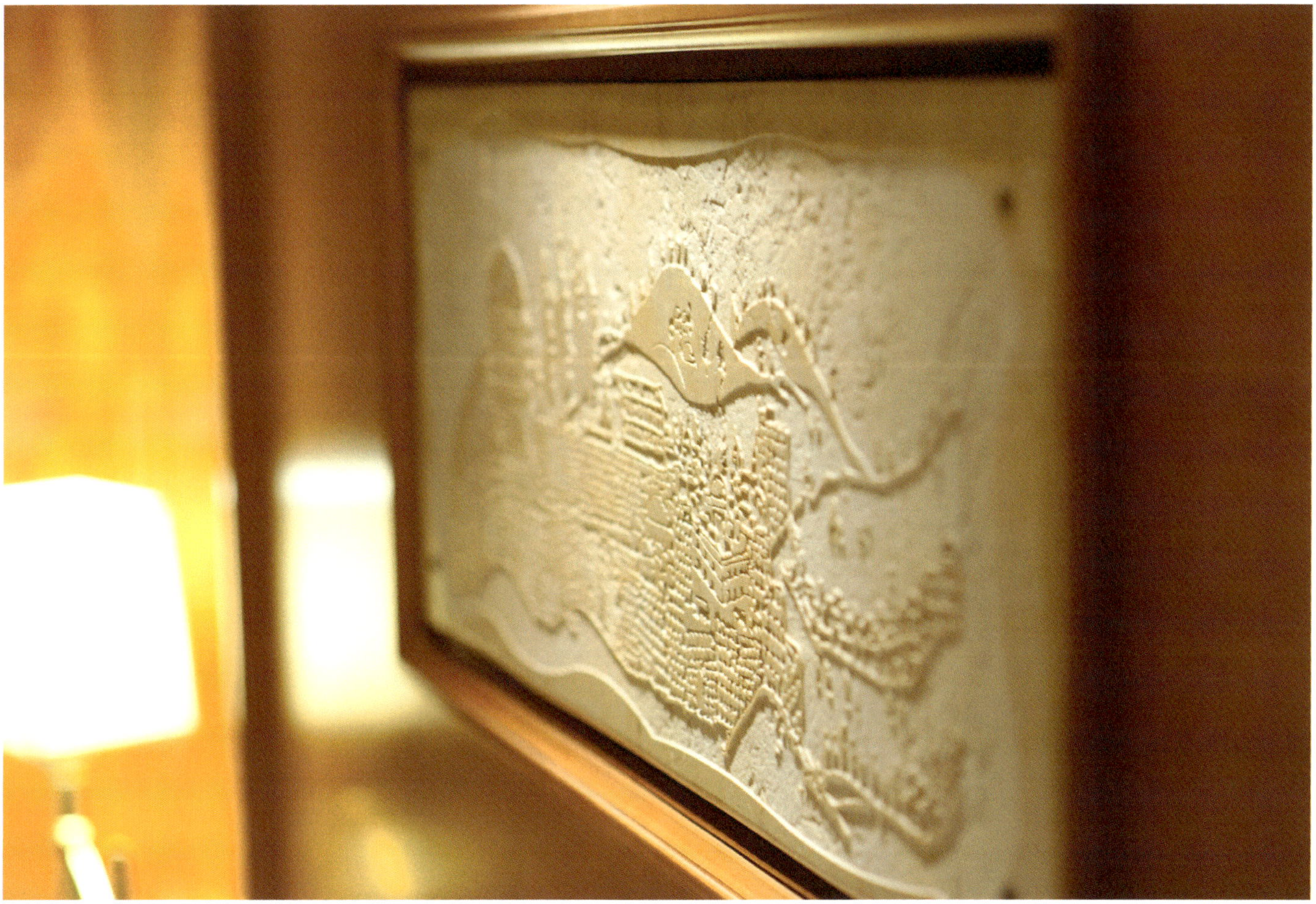

Above: **Carved image of ancient Jerusalem and the surrounding hills**

"For at that time I will change the speech of the peoples to a pure speech, that all of them may call upon the name of the LORD and serve Him with one accord. From beyond the rivers of Cush My worshipers, the daughter of My dispersed ones, shall bring My offering. 'On that day you shall not be put to shame because of the deeds by which you have rebelled against Me; for then I will remove from your midst your proudly exultant ones, and you shall no longer be haughty in My holy mountain. But I will leave in your midst a people humble and lowly. They shall seek refuge in the name of the LORD, those who are left in Israel; they shall do no injustice and speak no lies, nor shall there be found in their mouth a deceitful tongue. For they shall graze and lie down, and none shall make them afraid.'"

– Zephaniah 3:9-13 (ESV)

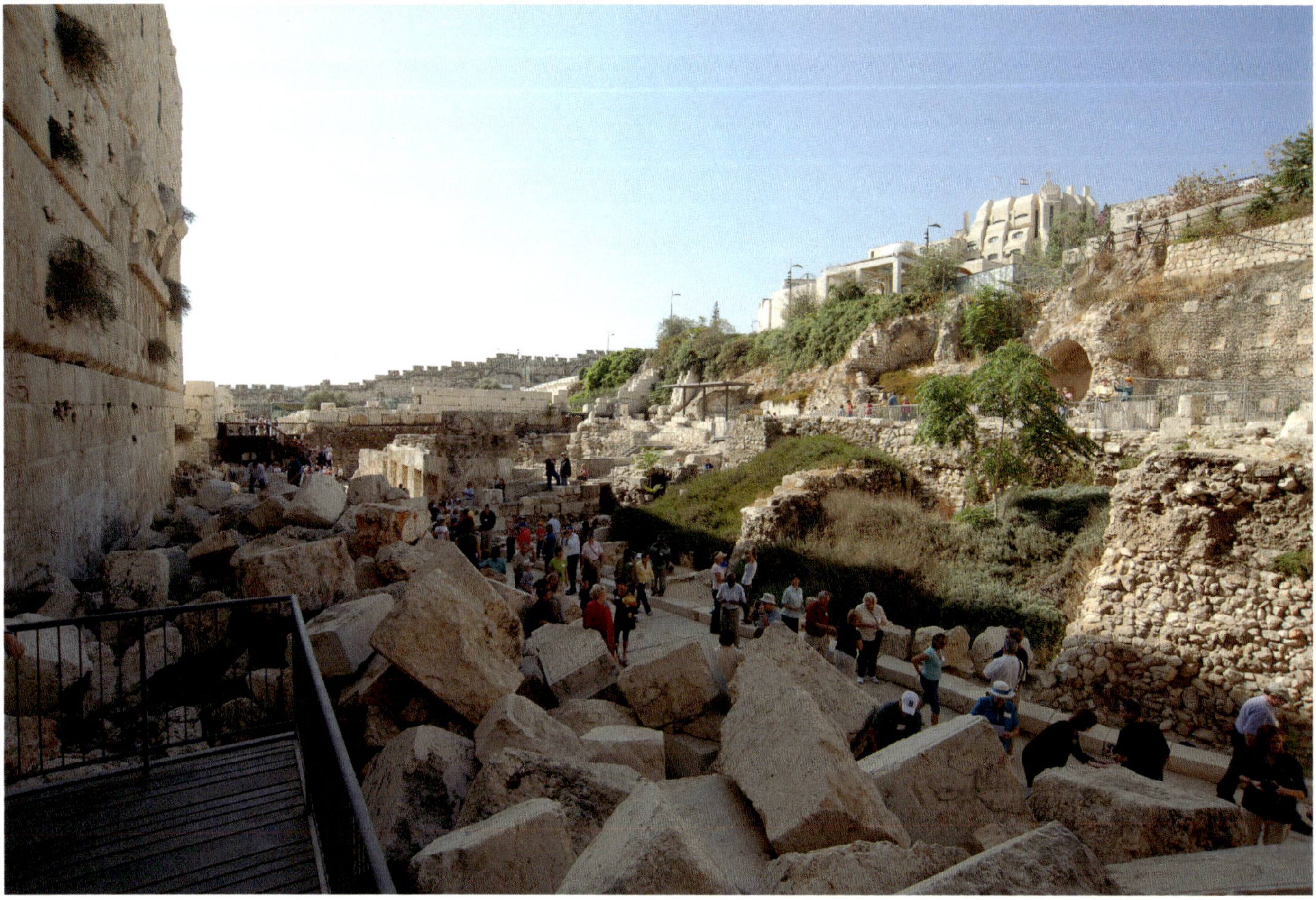

Above: **Excavation of the Western Wall of the Temple Mount**
The large stones are from the foundation of the temple itself. They were torn down and pushed off the mount when the Romans ransacked the city.

"Some of His disciples were remarking about how the temple was adorned with beautiful stones and with gifts dedicated to God. But Jesus said, 'As for what you see here, the time will come when not one stone will be left on another; every one of them will be thrown down. [...] when you see Jerusalem surrounded by armies, then know that its desolation has come near. Then let those who are in Judea flee to the mountains, and let those who are inside the city depart, and let not those who are out in the

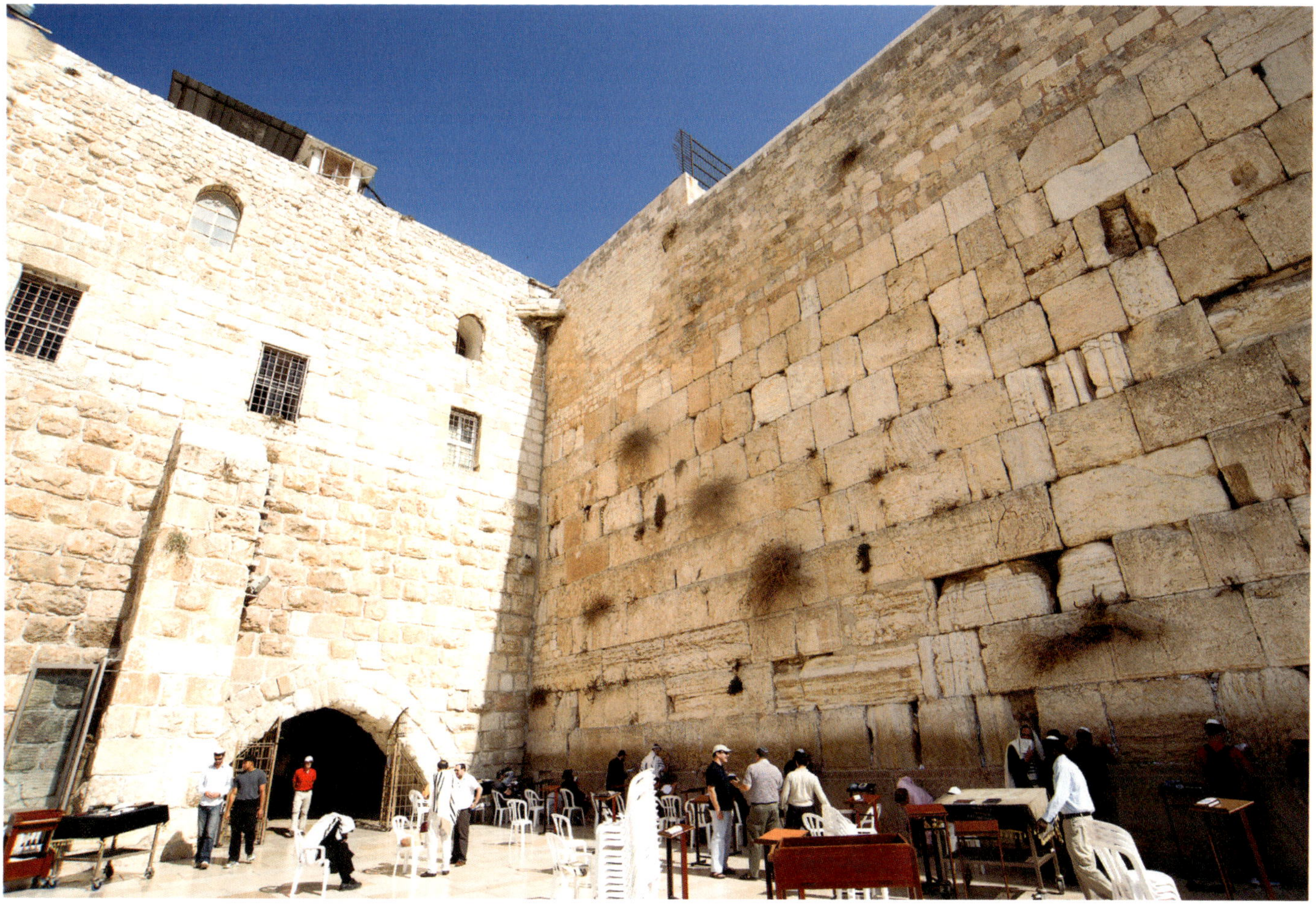

Above: **The Wailing Wall**
This section of the temple's western wall – one of the closest accessible sites to the temple's location – has long been a site of Jewish prayer and worship.

country enter it, for these are days of vengeance, to fulfill all that is written. Alas for women who are pregnant and for those who are nursing infants in those days! For there will be great distress upon the earth and wrath against this people. They will fall by the edge of the sword and be led captive among all nations, and Jerusalem will be trampled underfoot by the Gentiles, until the times of the Gentiles are fulfilled.'"

– Luke 21:5-6 (NIV), 20-24 (ESV)

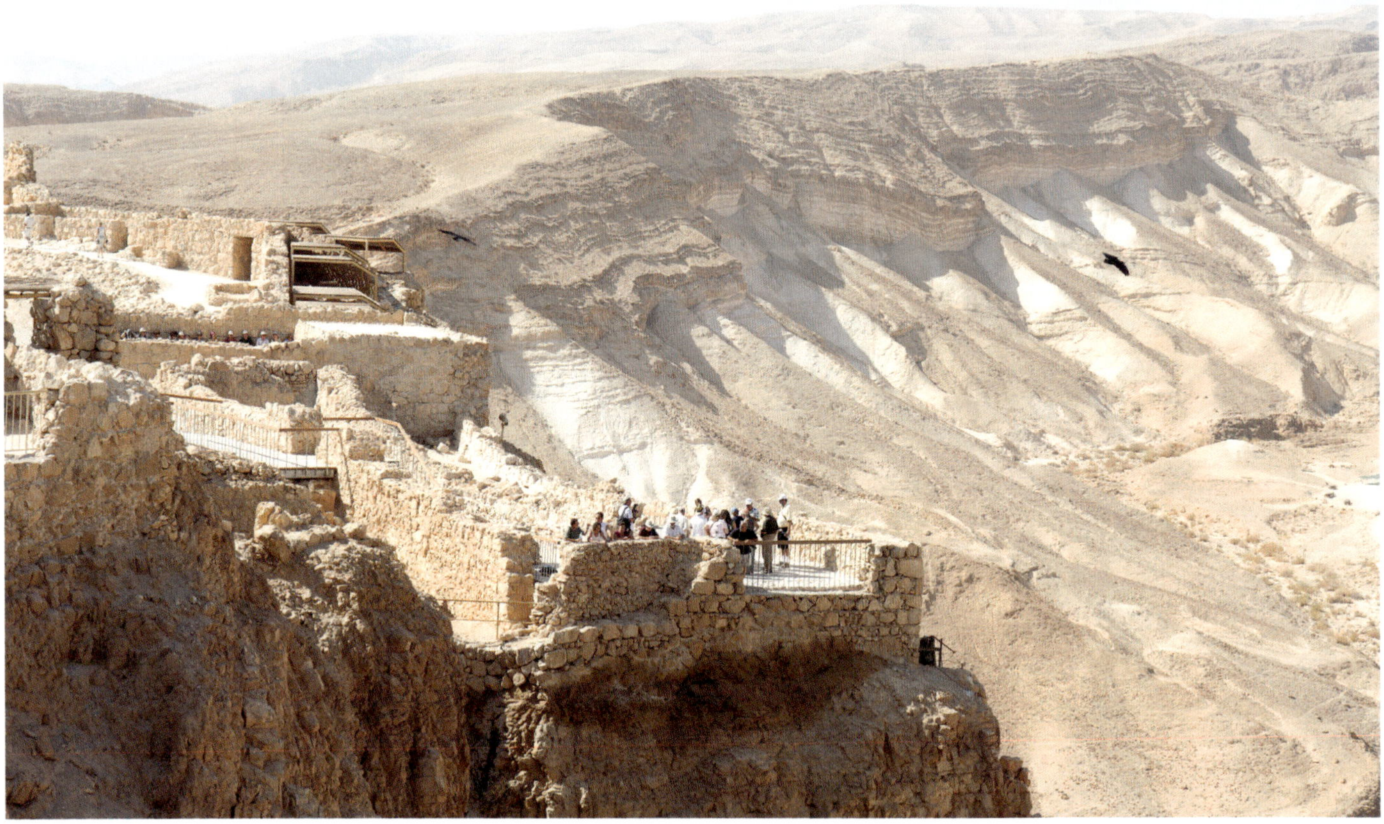

Above: **Masada**
Originally a palace for Herod the Great, this fortress was a refuge for Zealots fleeing the destruction of Jerusalem during the Jewish revolt against Rome.

"And when He drew near and saw the city, He wept over it, saying, 'Would that you, even you, had known on this day the things that make for peace! But now they are hidden from your eyes. For the days will come upon you, when your enemies will set up a barricade around you and surround you and hem you in on every side and tear you down to the ground, you and your children within you. And they will not leave one stone upon another in you, because you did not know the time of your visitation.'"

– Luke 19:41-44 (ESV)

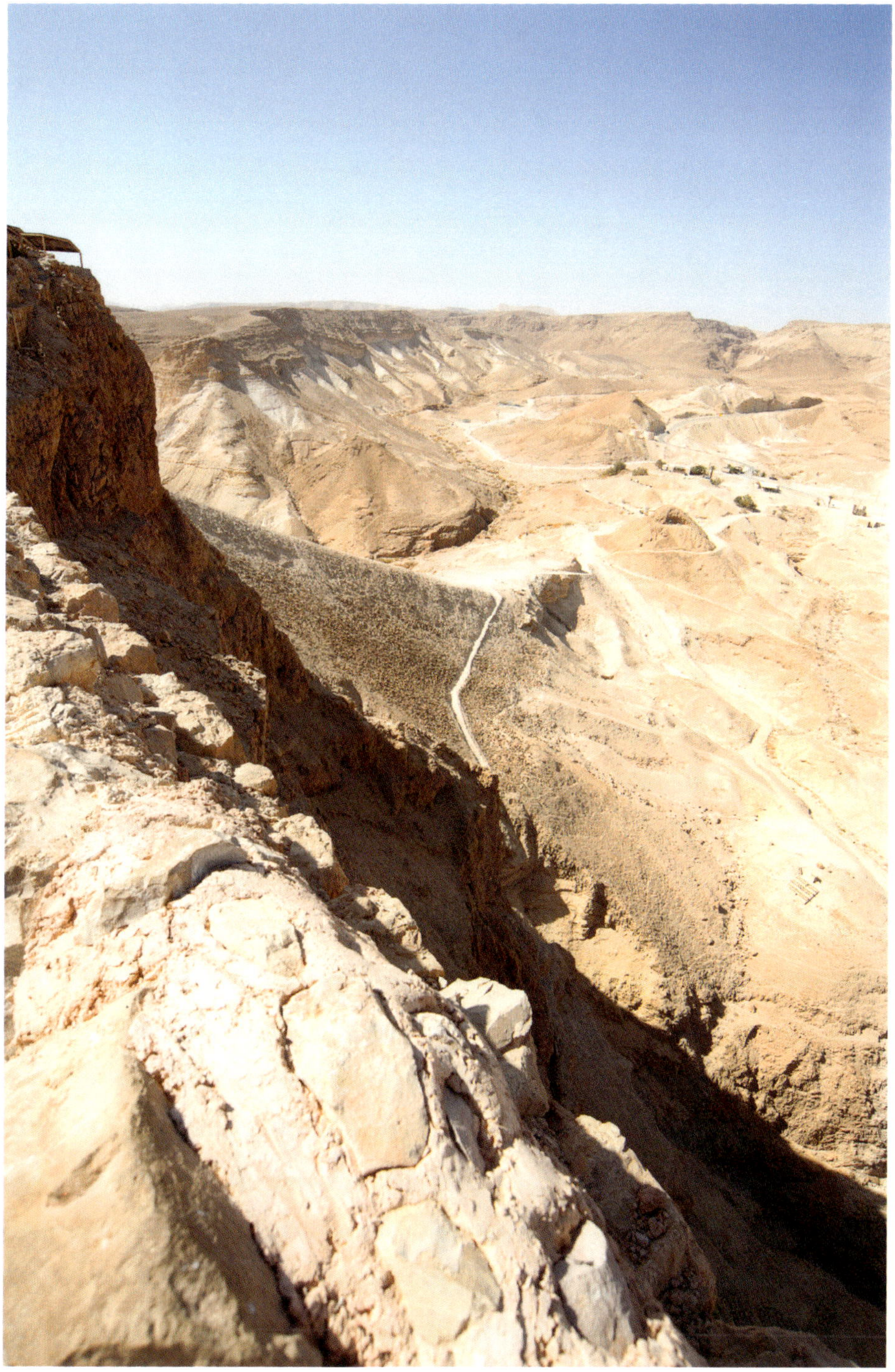

Above: **Roman siege ramp at Masada**
After surrounding the Jewish Zealots, the Romans built this ramp to assail the fortress's defenses. After breaching the wall, they found that the defenders had committed suicide rather than face capture. Today, soldiers are sworn into the Israeli Defense Forces atop the mountain with the pledge "Masada shall not fall again."

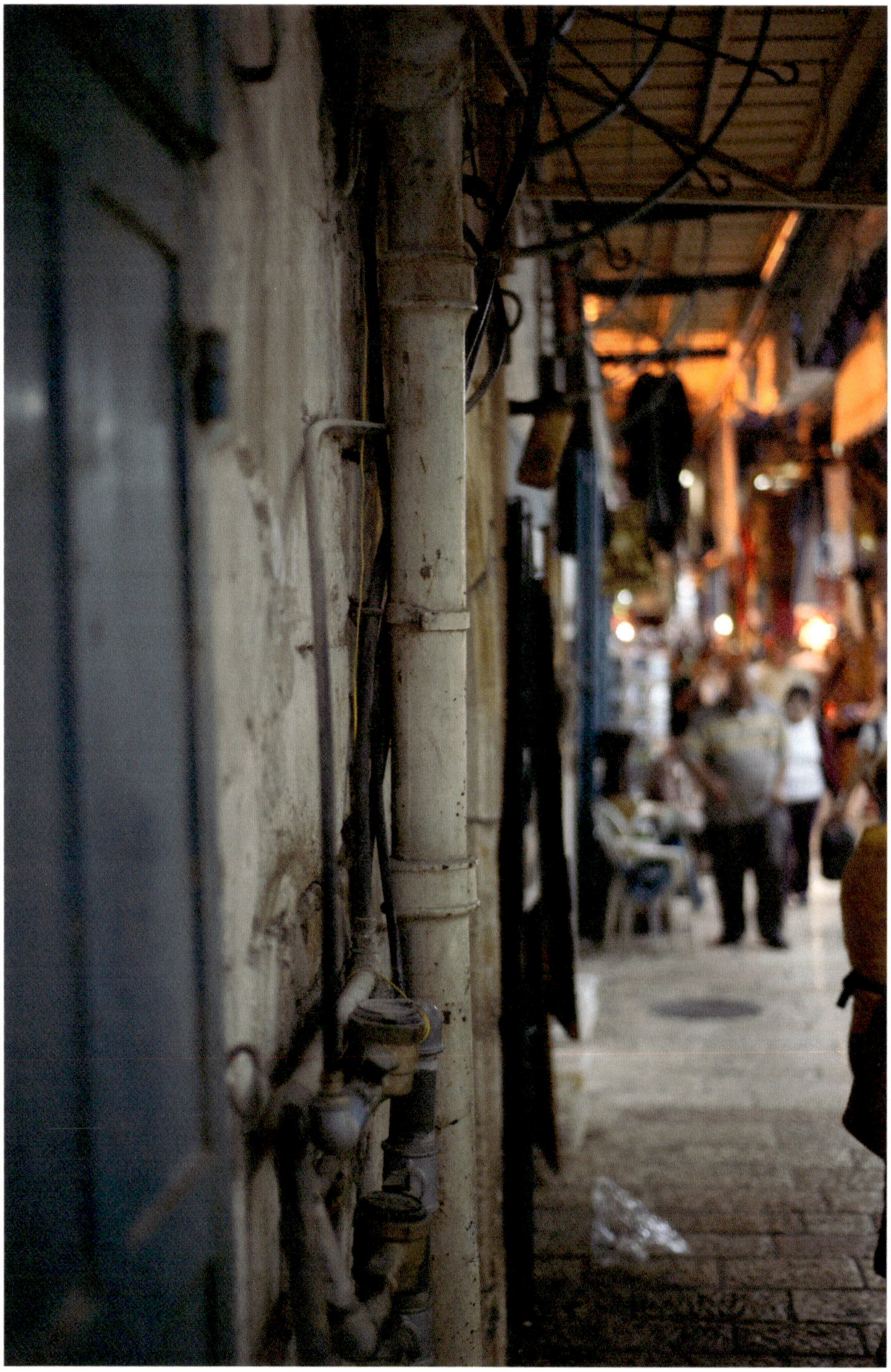

Pages 64-67: **The Jaffa Gate market in the Old City of Jerusalem**

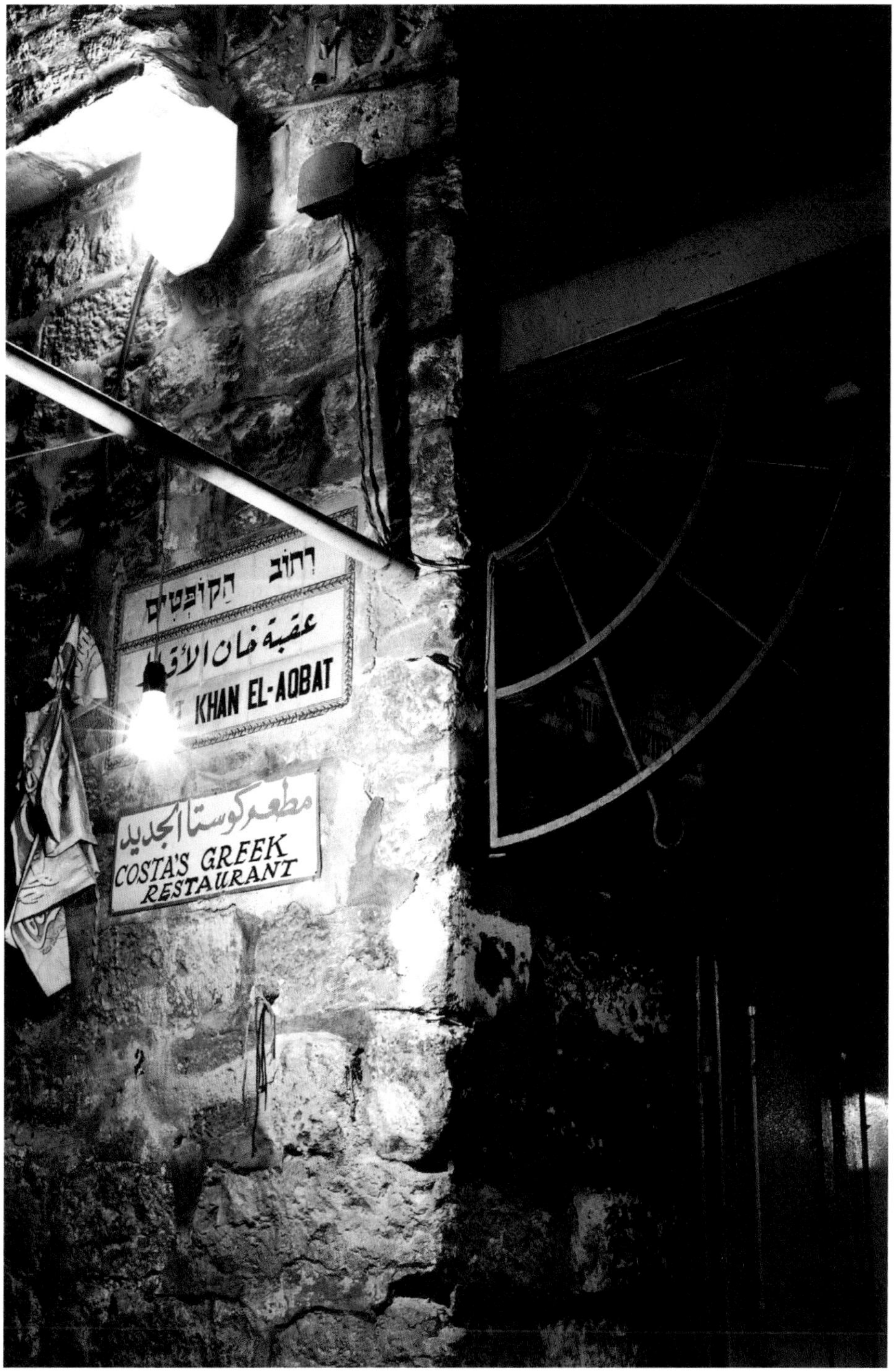

"For Zion's sake I will not keep silent, and for Jerusalem's sake I will not be quiet, until her righteousness goes forth as brightness, and her salvation as a burning torch. The nations shall see your righteousness, and all the kings your glory, and you shall be called by a new name that the mouth of the LORD will give. You shall be a crown of beauty in the hand of the LORD, and a royal diadem in the hand of your God. You shall no more be termed Forsaken, and your land shall no more be termed Desolate, but you

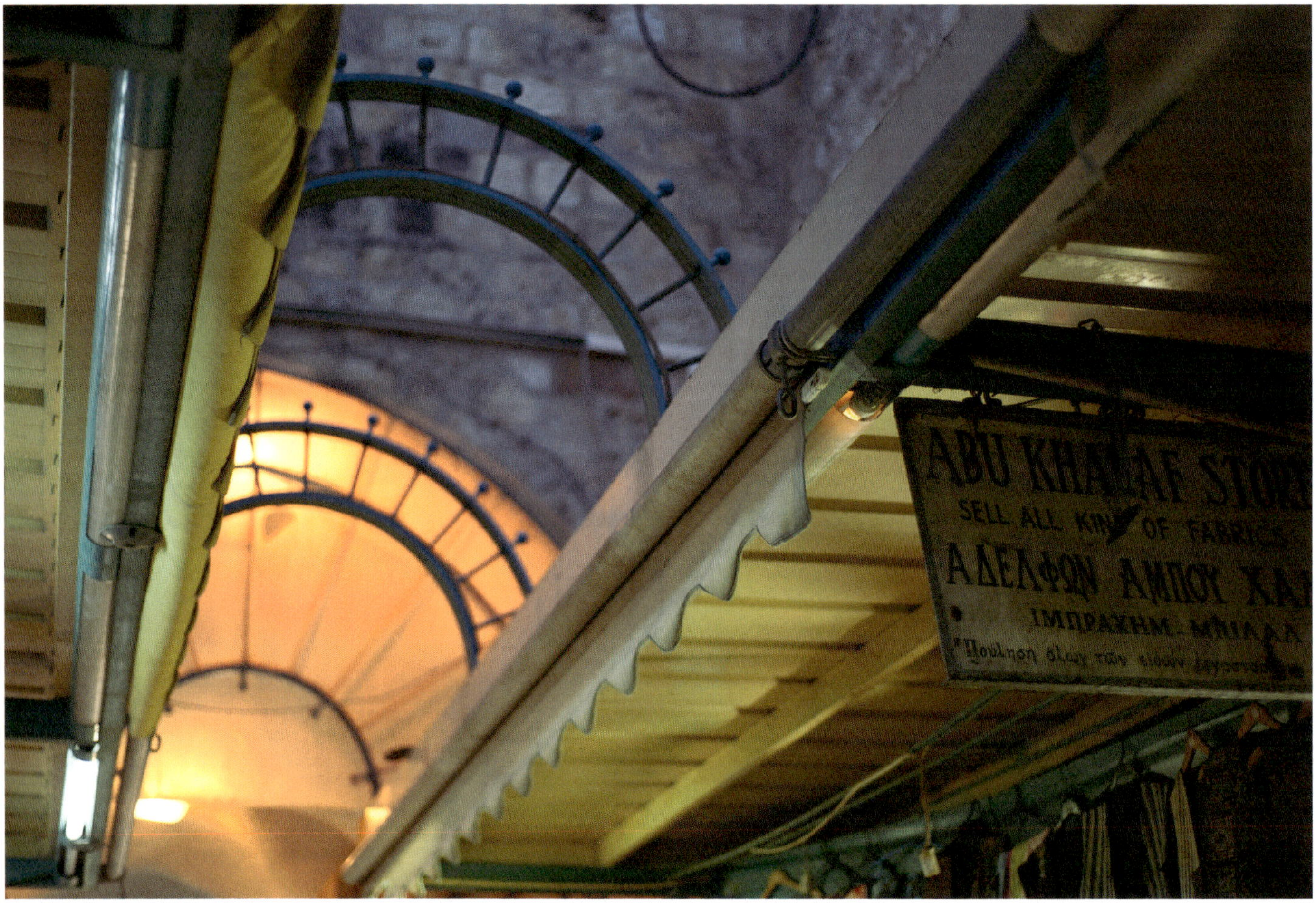

shall be called My Delight Is in Her, and your land Married; for the LORD delights in you, and your land shall be married. For as a young man marries a young woman, so shall your sons marry you, and as the bridegroom rejoices over the bride, so shall your God rejoice over you. On your walls, O Jerusalem, I have set watchmen; all the day and all the night they shall never be silent. You who put the LORD in remembrance, take no rest, and give him no rest until he establishes Jerusalem and makes it a praise in the earth. The LORD has sworn by his right hand and by his mighty arm: 'I will not again give your grain to be food for your enemies, and foreigners shall not drink your wine for which you have labored; but those who garner it shall eat it and praise the LORD, and those who gather it shall drink it in the courts of my sanctuary.' Go through, go through the gates; prepare the way for the people; build up, build up the highway; clear it of stones; lift up a signal over the peoples. Behold, the LORD has proclaimed to

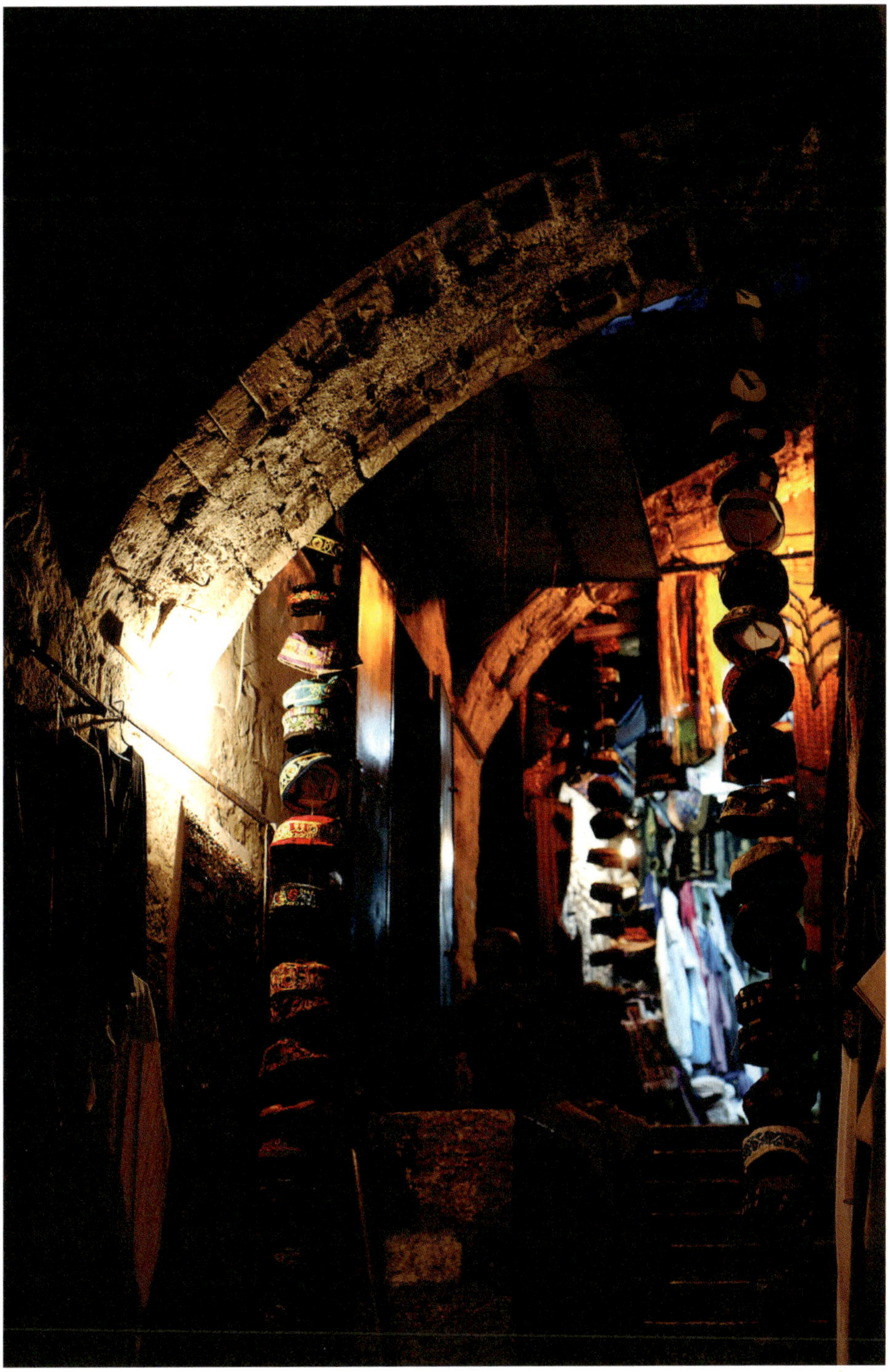

the end of the earth: Say to the daughter of Zion, 'Behold, your salvation comes; behold, his reward is with him, and his recompense before him.' And they shall be called The Holy People, The Redeemed of the LORD; and you shall be called Sought Out, A City Not Forsaken."

– Isaiah 62 (ESV)

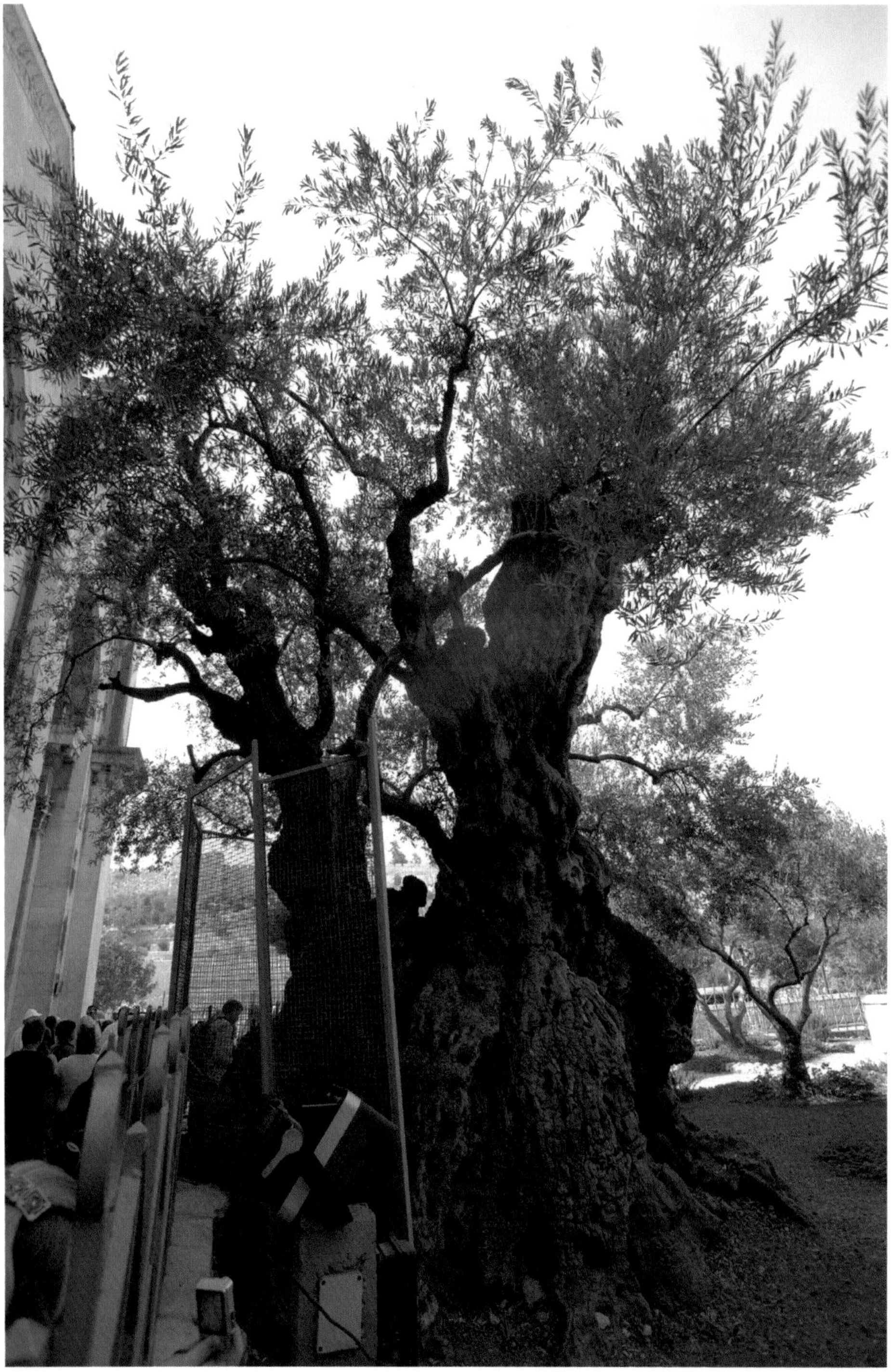

Above: **Olive tree in the Garden of Gethsemane**
Olive trees can grow to be very old, living perhaps as long as four thousand years. This particular tree is centuries old and possibly a witness to the events described below.

"Then Jesus went with His disciples to a place called Gethsemane, and He said to them, 'Sit here while I go over there and pray.' He took Peter and the two sons of Zebedee along with Him, and He began to be sorrowful and troubled. Then He said to them, 'My soul is overwhelmed with sorrow to the point of death. Stay here and keep watch with Me.' Going a little farther, He fell with His face to the ground and prayed, 'My Father, if it is possible, may this cup be taken from Me. Yet not as I will, but as you will.' Then He returned to His disciples and found them sleeping. 'Could you men not keep watch with Me for one hour?' He asked Peter. 'Watch and pray so that you will not fall into temptation. The spirit is willing, but the body is weak.' He went away a second time and prayed, 'My Father, if it is not possible for this cup to be taken away unless I drink it, may Your will be done.' When He came back, He again found them sleeping, because their eyes were heavy. So He left them and went away once more and prayed the third time, saying the same thing. Then He returned to the disciples and said to them, 'Are you still sleeping and resting? Look, the hour is near, and the Son of Man is betrayed into the hands of sinners. Rise, let us go! Here comes my betrayer!'"

– Matthew 26:36-46 (NIV)

"So when Pilate saw that he was gaining nothing, but rather that a riot was beginning, he took water and washed his hands before the crowd, saying, 'I am innocent of this man's blood; see to it yourselves.' And all the people answered, 'His blood be on us and on our children!' Then he released for them Barabbas, and having scourged Jesus, delivered Him to be crucified. Then the soldiers of the governor took Jesus into the governor's headquarters, and they gathered the whole battalion before Him. And they stripped Him and put a scarlet robe on Him, and twisting together a crown of thorns, they put it on His head and put a reed in His right hand. And kneeling before Him, they mocked Him, saying, 'Hail, King of the Jews!' And they spit on Him and took the reed and struck Him on the head. And when they had mocked Him, they stripped Him of the robe and put His own clothes on Him and led Him away to crucify Him."

– Matthew 27:24-31 (ESV)

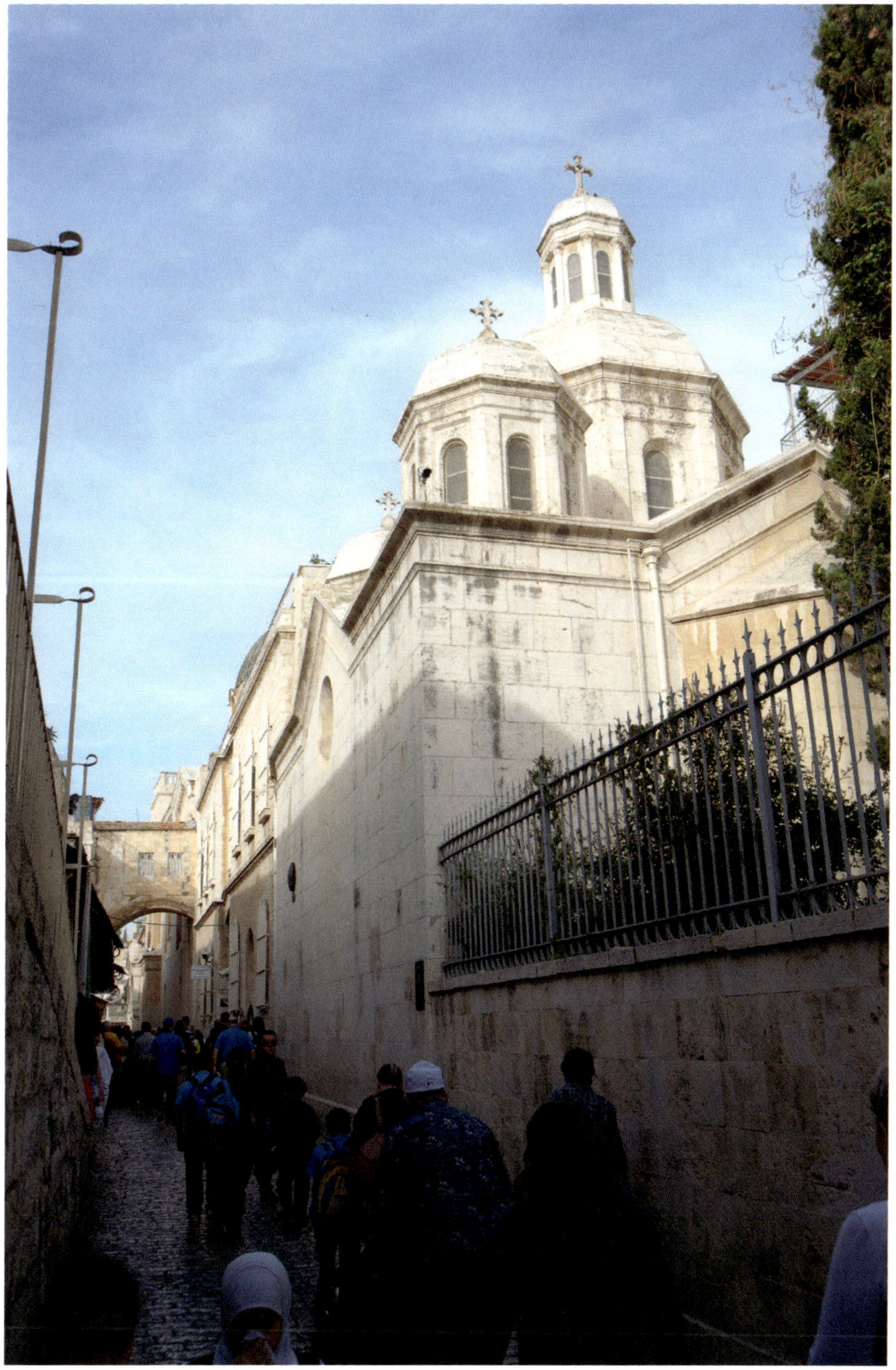

Above: **Ecce Homo Church and Convent**
The church is a station on the Via Dolorosa, the traditional route that Jesus followed to His crucifixion.

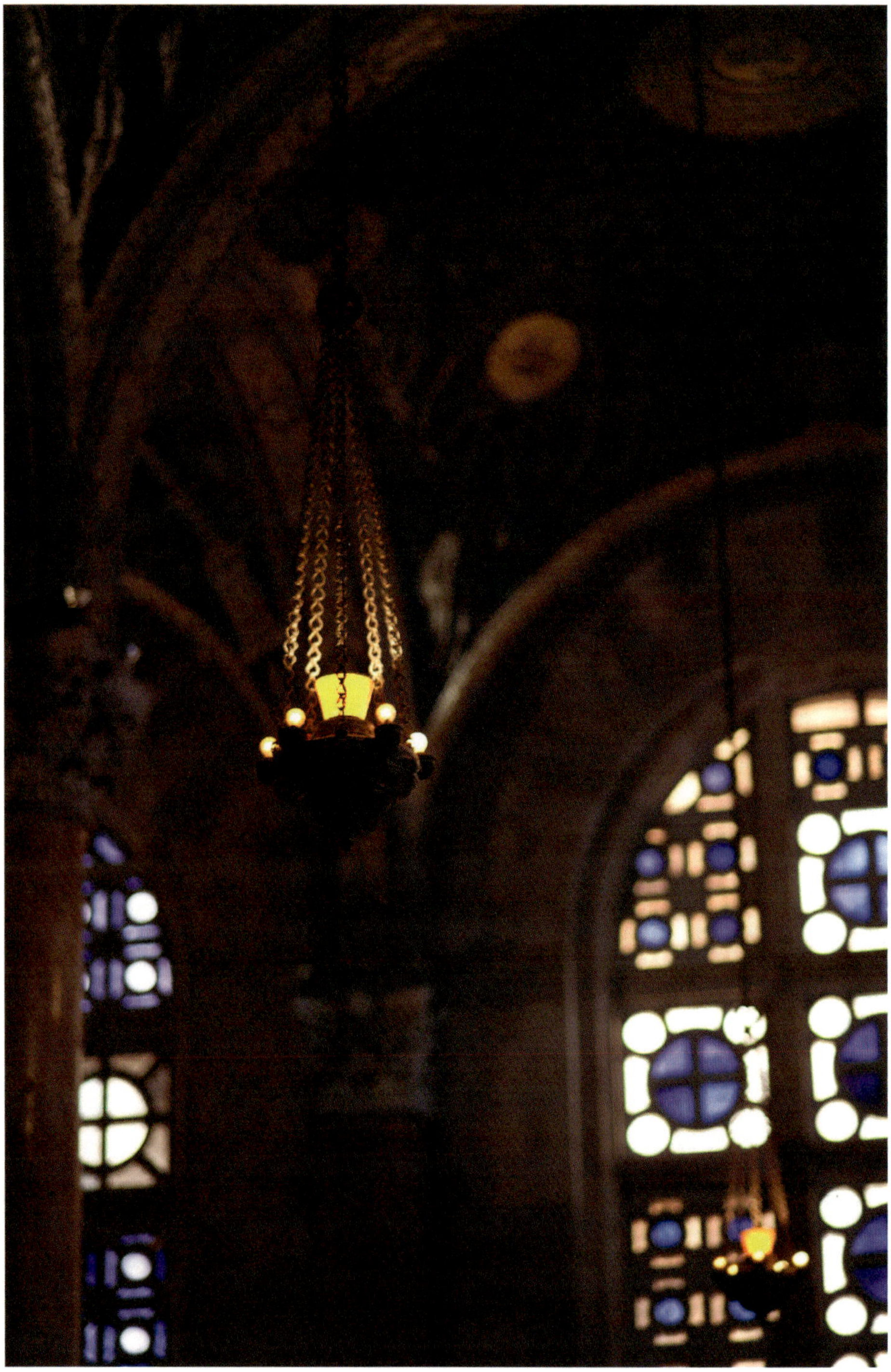

Above: **The interior of the Church of All Nations in the Garden of Gethsemane**

Right: **A skull-shaped rock outcropping near the Garden Tomb**
This is a possible location of *Golgatha* (the Place of the Skull) where Jesus's crucifixion took place.

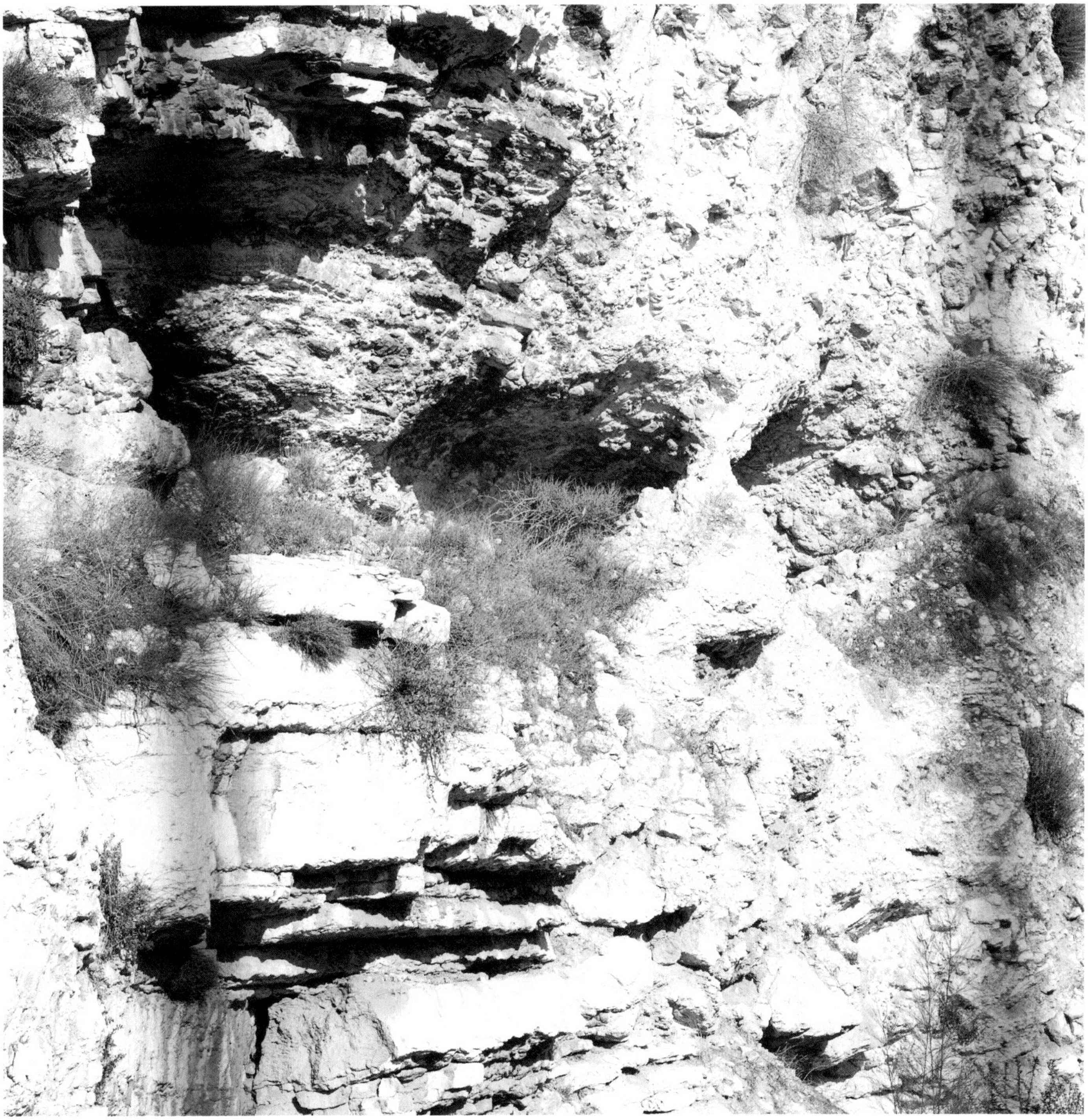

"…So they took Jesus, and He went out, bearing His own cross, to the place called The Place of a Skull, which in Aramaic is called Golgotha. There they crucified Him, and with Him two others, one on either side, and Jesus between them. Pilate also wrote an inscription and put it on the cross. It read, 'Jesus of Nazareth, the King of the Jews.' Many of the Jews read this inscription, for the place where Jesus was crucified was near the city, and it was written in Aramaic, in Latin, and in Greek. So the chief priests of the Jews said to Pilate, 'Do not write, 'The King of the Jews,' but rather, 'This man said, I am King of the Jews.''' Pilate answered, 'What I have written I have written.'"

– John 19:16-22 (ESV)

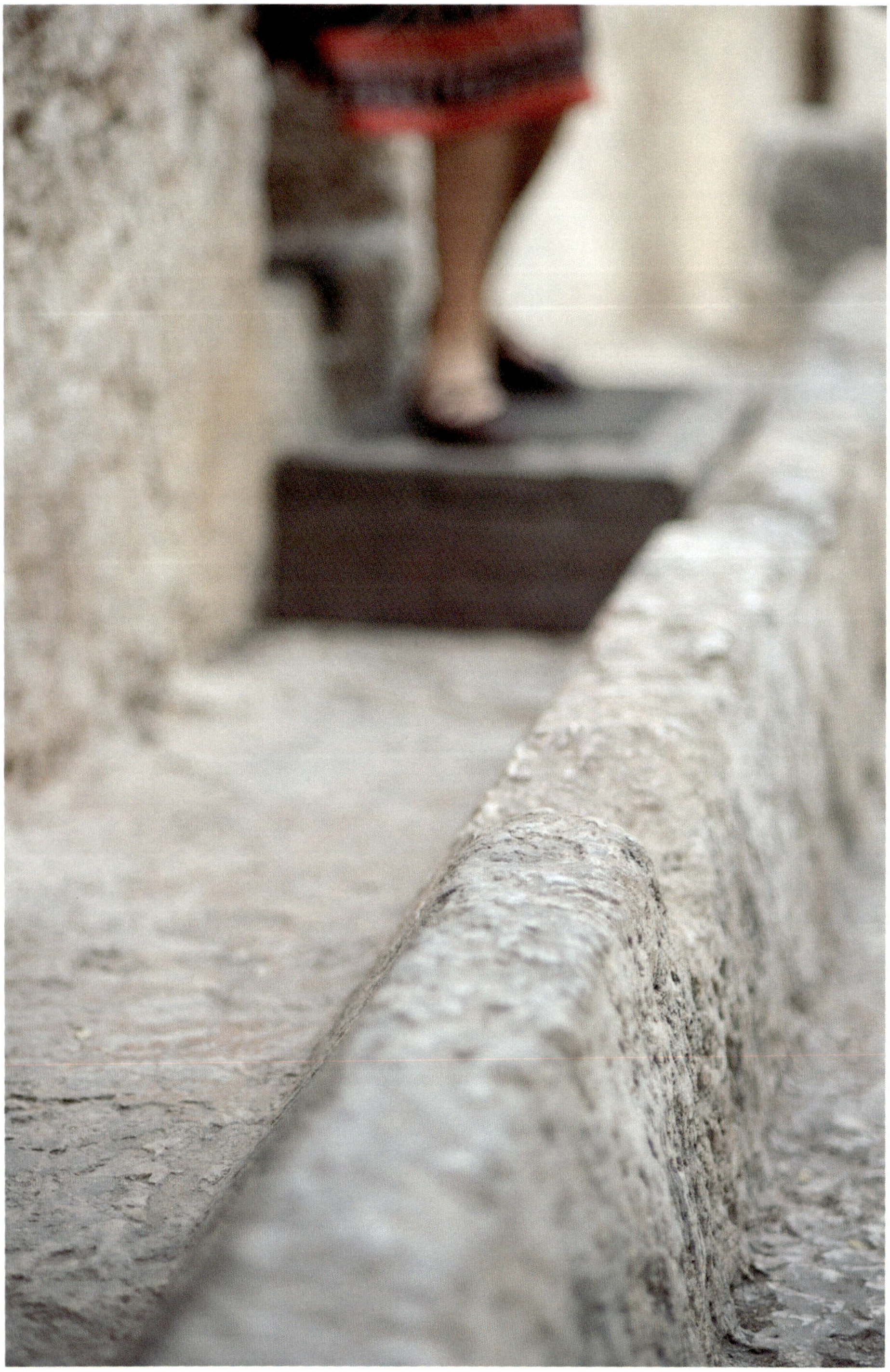

Pages 72 and 73: **The Garden Tomb in Jerusalem**

"And those who passed by derided Him [Jesus], wagging their heads and saying, 'Aha! You who would destroy the temple and rebuild it in three days, save Yourself, and come down from the cross!' So also the chief priests with the scribes mocked Him to one another, saying, 'He saved others; He cannot save Himself. Let the Christ, the King of Israel, come down now from the cross that we may see and believe.' Those who were crucified with Him also reviled Him. And when the sixth hour had come, there was darkness over the whole land until the ninth hour. And at the ninth hour Jesus cried with a loud voice, 'Eloi, Eloi, lema sabachthani?' which means, 'My God, my God, why have you forsaken me?' And some of the bystanders hearing it said, 'Behold, he is calling Elijah.' And someone ran and filled a sponge with sour wine, put it on a reed and gave it to Him to drink, saying, 'Wait, let us see whether Elijah will come to take Him down.' And Jesus uttered a loud cry and breathed His last. And the curtain of the temple was torn in two, from top to bottom. And when the centurion, who stood facing Him, saw that in this way He breathed His last, he said, 'Truly this man was the Son of God!' There were also women looking on from a distance, among whom were Mary Magdalene, and Mary the mother of James the younger and of Joses, and Salome. When he was in Galilee, they followed Him and ministered to Him, and there were also many other women who came up with Him to Jerusalem. And when evening had come, since it was the day of Preparation, that is, the day before the Sabbath, Joseph of Arimathea, a respected member of the Council, who was also himself looking for the kingdom of God, took courage and went to Pilate and asked for the body of Jesus. Pilate was surprised to hear that He should have already died. And summoning the centurion, he asked him whether He was already dead. And when he learned from the centurion that He was dead, he granted the corpse to Joseph. And Joseph bought a linen shroud, and taking Him down, wrapped Him in the linen shroud and laid Him in a tomb that had been cut out of the rock. And he rolled a stone against the entrance of the tomb. Mary Magdalene and Mary the mother of Joses saw where He was laid. When the Sabbath was past, Mary Magdalene and Mary the mother of James and Salome bought spices, so that they might go and anoint Him. And very early on the first day of the week, when the sun had risen, they went to the tomb. And they were saying to one another, 'Who will roll away the stone for us from the entrance of the tomb?' And looking up, they saw that the stone had been rolled back – it was very large. And entering the tomb, they saw a young man sitting on the right side, dressed in a white robe, and they were alarmed. And he said to them, 'Do not be alarmed. You seek Jesus of Nazareth, who

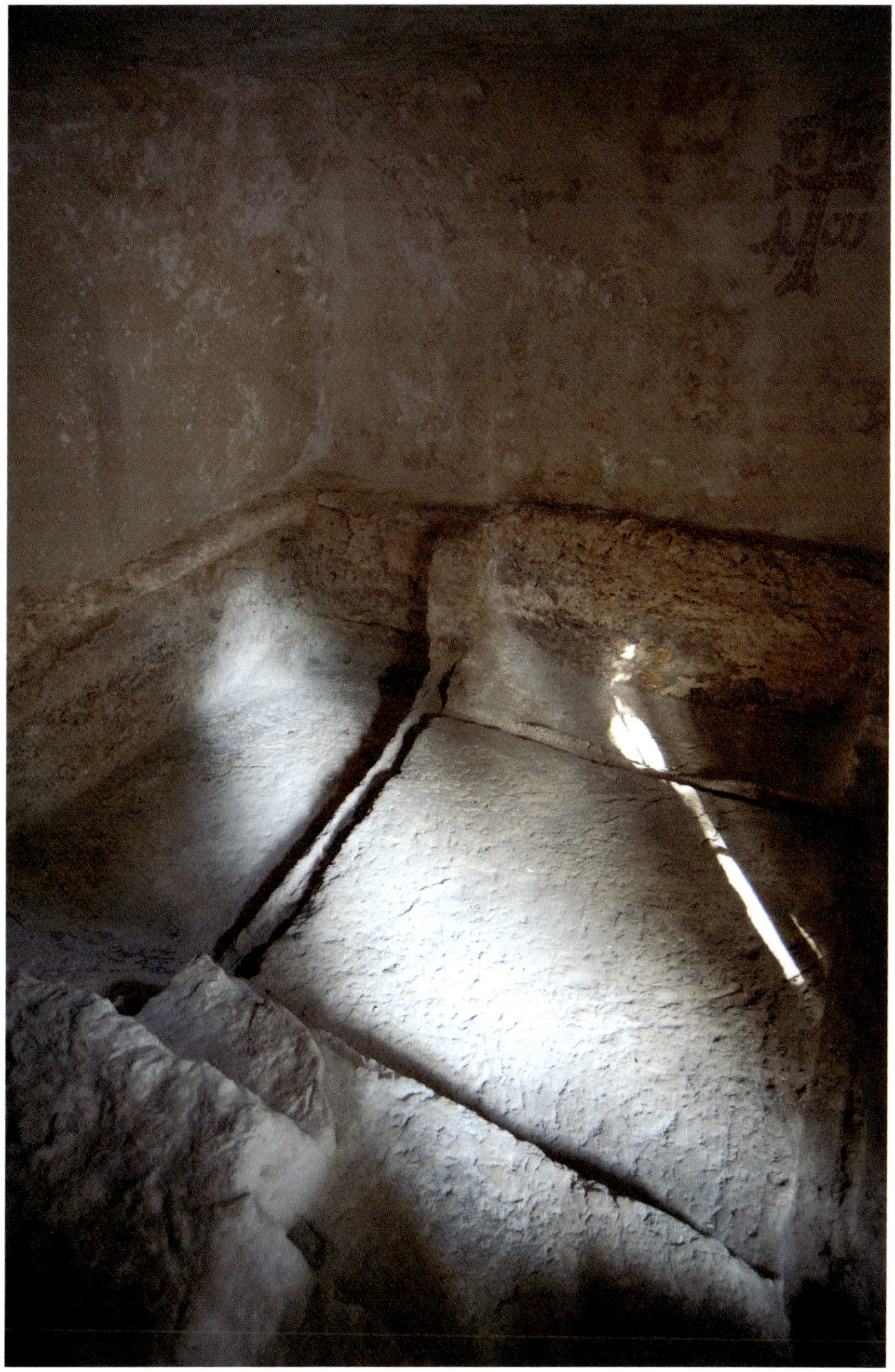

was crucified. He has risen; He is not here. See the place where they laid Him. But go, tell His disciples and Peter that He is going before you to Galilee. There you will see Him, just as He told you.' And they went out and fled from the tomb, for trembling and astonishment had seized them, and they said nothing to anyone, for they were afraid."

– Mark 15:29-16:8 (ESV)

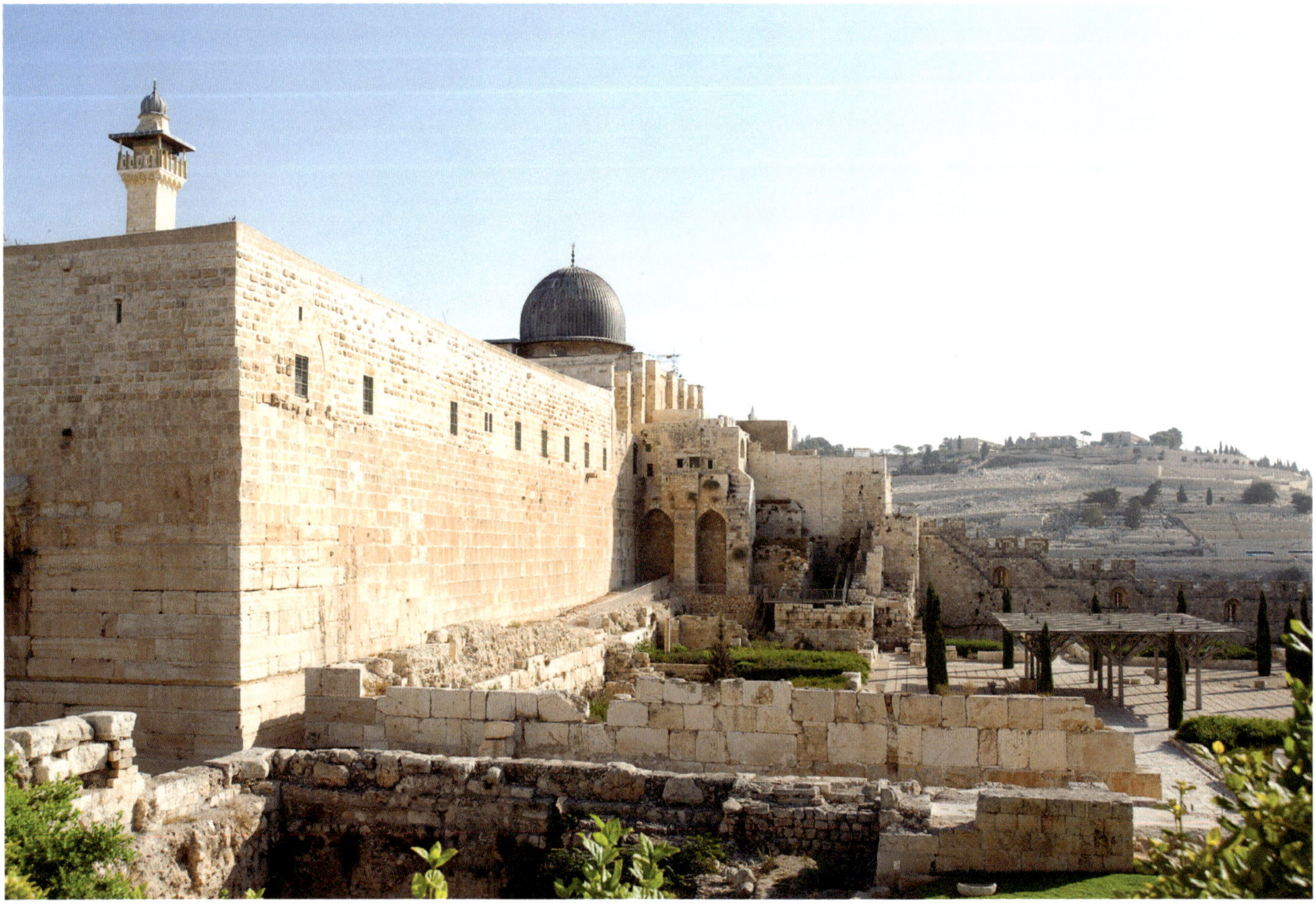

Above: **The southern stairs of the Temple Mount**
The Mount of Olives is in the background.

"Now Peter and John were going up to the temple at the hour of prayer, the ninth hour. And a man lame from birth was being carried, whom they laid daily at the gate of the temple that is called the Beautiful Gate to ask alms of those entering the temple. Seeing Peter and John about to go into the temple, he asked to receive alms. And Peter directed his gaze at him, as did John, and said, 'Look at us.' And he fixed his attention on them, expecting to receive something from them. But Peter said, 'I have no silver and gold, but what I do have I give to you. In the name of Jesus Christ of Nazareth, rise up and walk!'"

– Acts 3:1-6 (ESV)

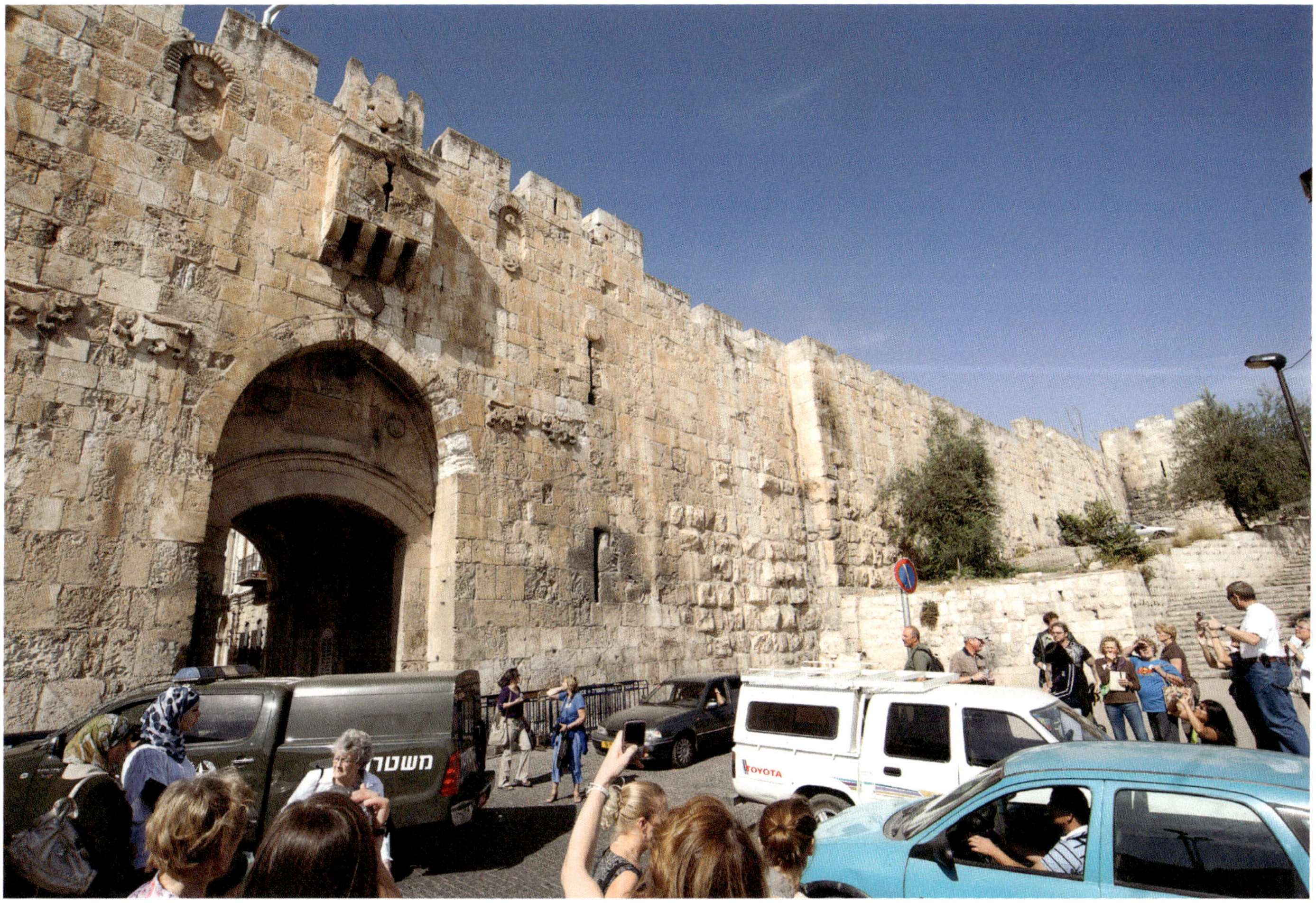

Above: **The Lions' Gate**
This gate is traditionally known as the place of St. Stephen's martyrdom, although its position is somewhat different from the gate that existed at Stephen's time.

"Now when they heard these things they were enraged, and they ground their teeth at him [Stephen]. But he, full of the Holy Spirit, gazed into heaven and saw the glory of God, and Jesus standing at the right hand of God. And he said, 'Behold, I see the heavens opened, and the Son of Man standing at the right hand of God.' But they cried out with a loud voice and stopped their ears and rushed together at him. Then they cast him out of the city and stoned him. And the witnesses laid down their garments at the feet of a young man named Saul. And as they were stoning Stephen, he called out, 'Lord Jesus, receive my spirit.' And falling to his knees he cried out with a loud voice, 'Lord, do not hold this sin against them.' And when he had said this, he fell asleep."

– Acts 7:54-60 (ESV)

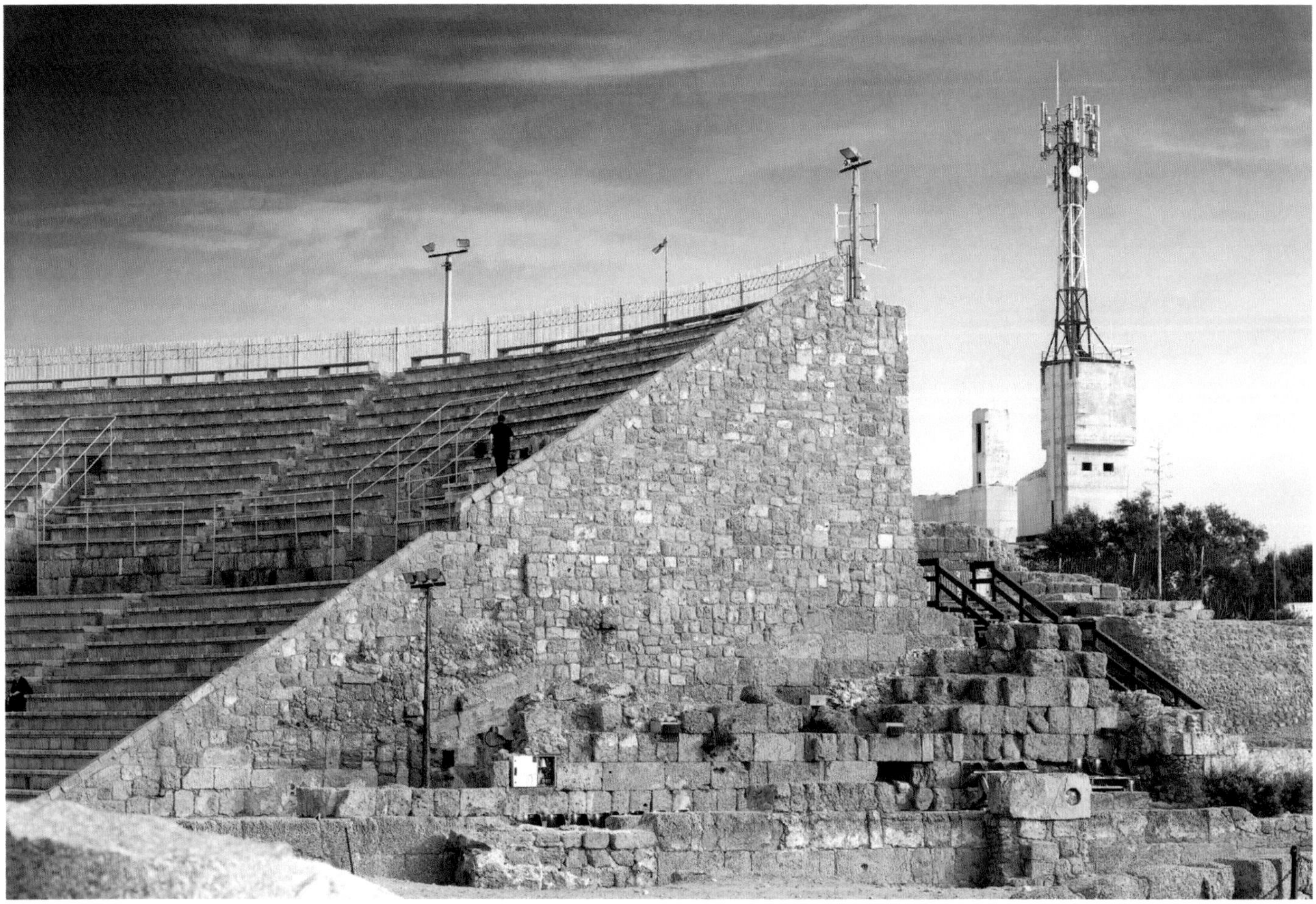

Pages 76 and 77: **Caesarea**
Caesarea was a major Roman port and administrative center.
Paul was held as a prisoner here before being sent to Rome.

"'First to those in Damascus, then to those in Jerusalem and in all Judea, and to the Gentiles also, I preached that they should repent and turn to God and prove their repentance by their deeds. That is why the Jews seized me in the temple courts and tried to kill me. But I have had God's help to this very day, and so I stand here and testify to small and great alike. I am saying nothing beyond what the prophets and Moses said would happen – that the Christ would suffer and, as the first to rise from the dead, would proclaim light to his own people and to the Gentiles.' At this point Festus interrupted Paul's defense. 'You are out of your mind, Paul!' he shouted. 'Your great learning is driving you insane.'

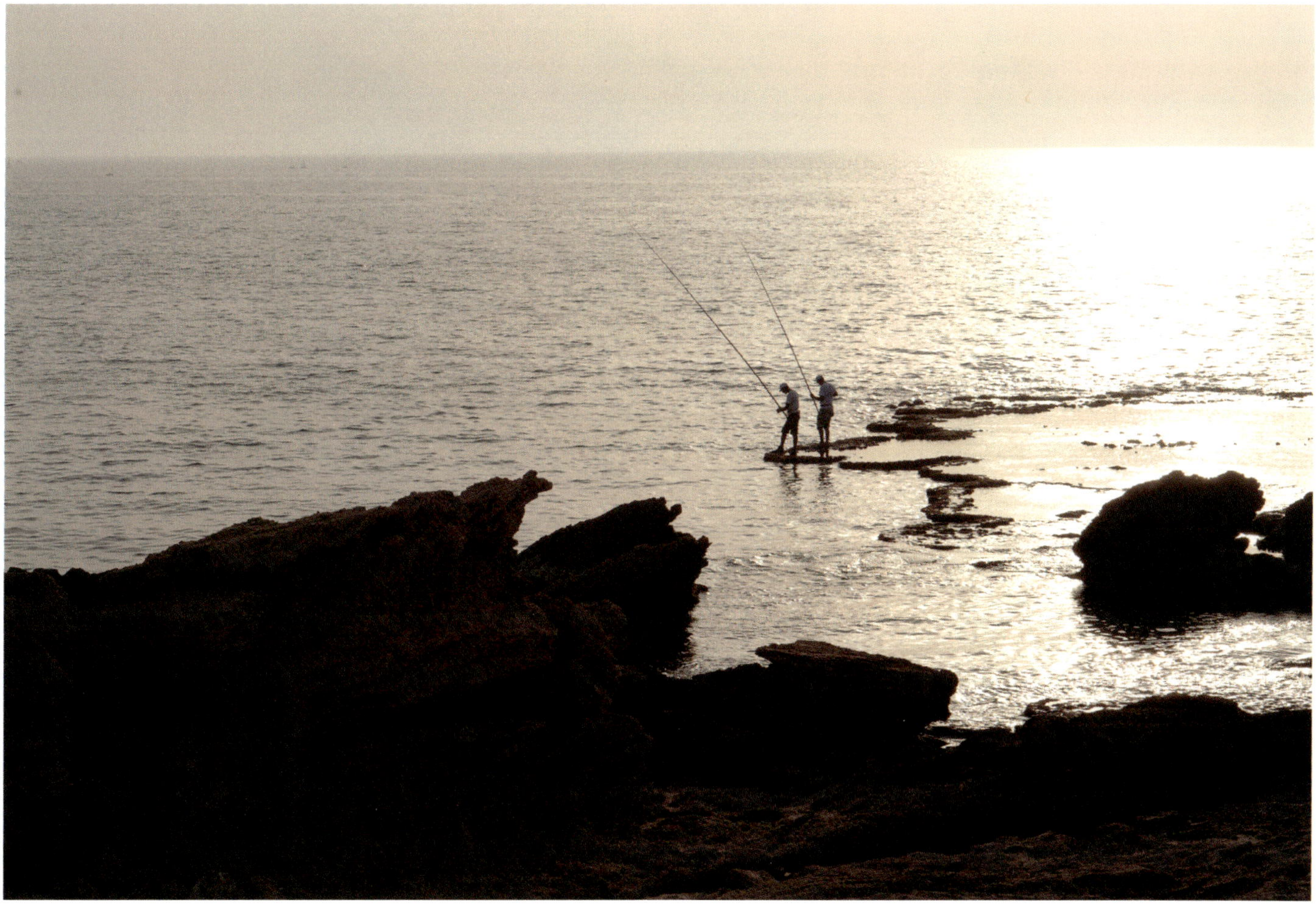

'I am not insane, most excellent Festus,' Paul replied. 'What I am saying is true and reasonable. The king is familiar with these things, and I can speak freely to him. I am convinced that none of this has escaped his notice, because it was not done in a corner. King Agrippa, do you believe the prophets? I know you do.' Then Agrippa said to Paul, 'Do you think that in such a short time you can persuade me to be a Christian?' Paul replied, 'Short time or long – I pray to God that not only you but all who are listening to me today may become what I am, except for these chains.'"

– Acts 26:20-29 (NIV)

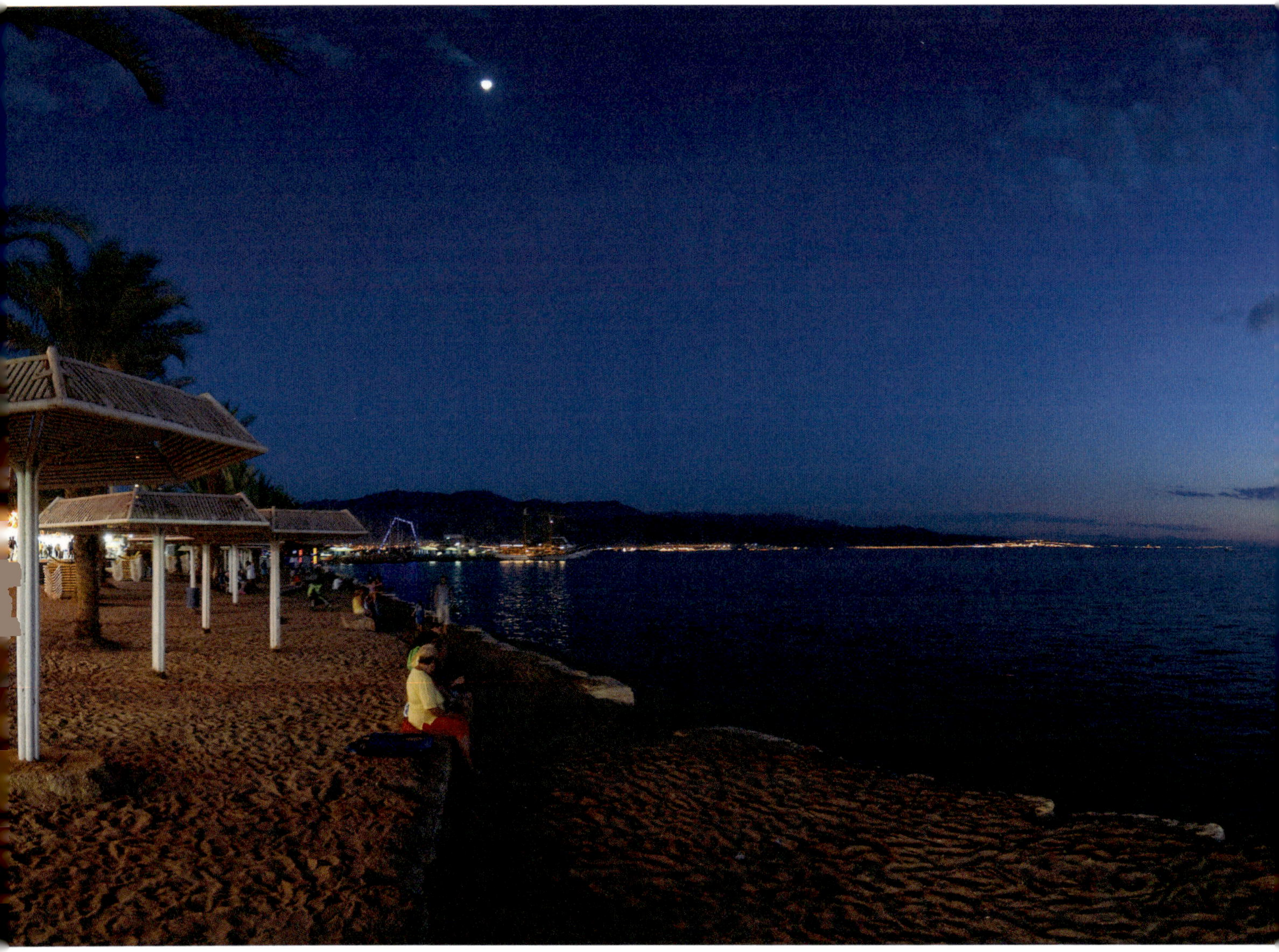

Above: **Four nations**
From the left to the right they are Jordan, Saudi Arabia, and Egypt.
The picture was taken from the southern tip of Israel at Eliat.

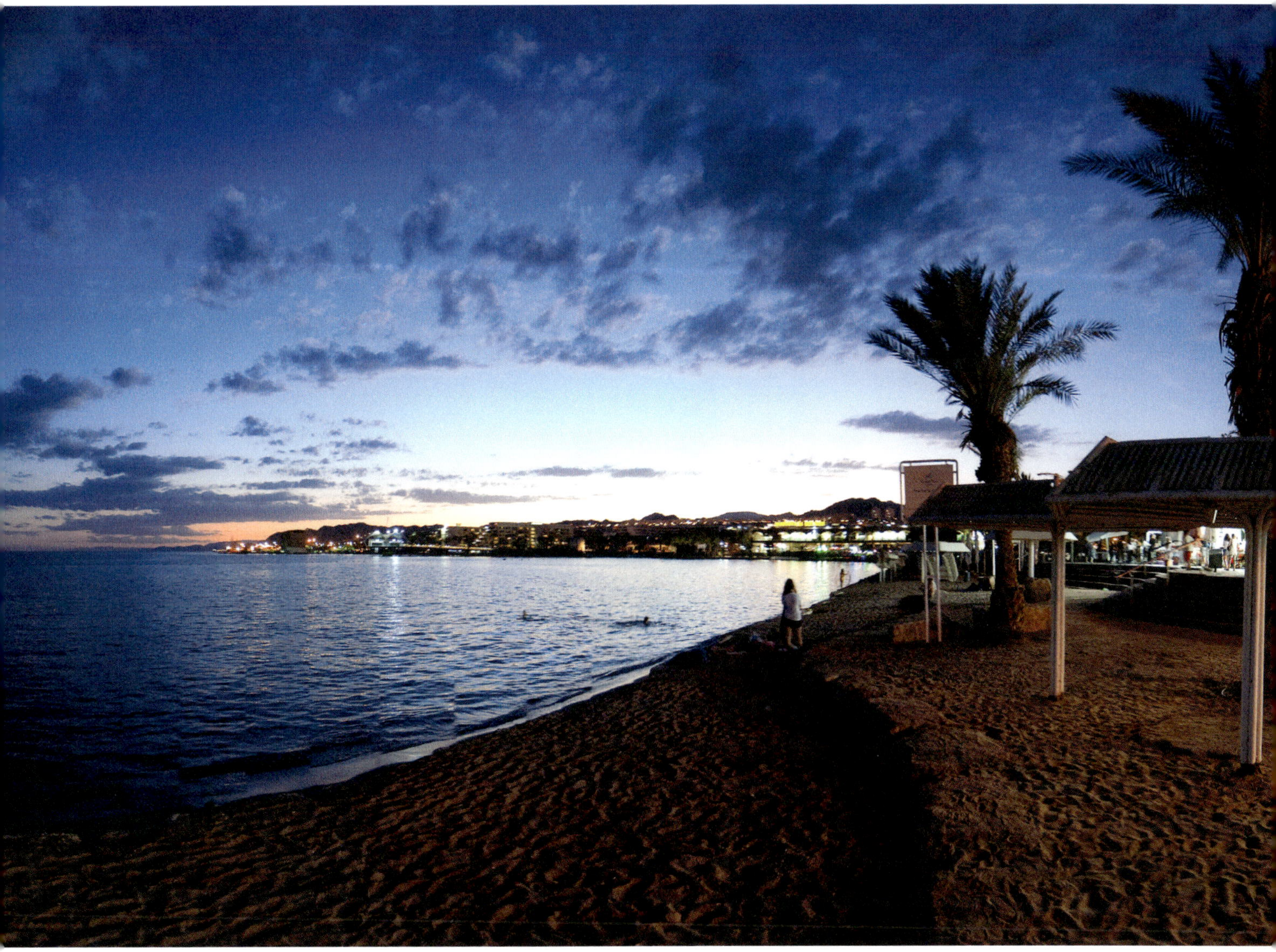

"Go therefore and make disciples of all nations, baptizing them in the name of the Father and of the Son and of the Holy Spirit, teaching them to observe all that I have commanded you. And behold, I am with you always, to the end of the age."

– Matthew 28:19-20 (ESV)

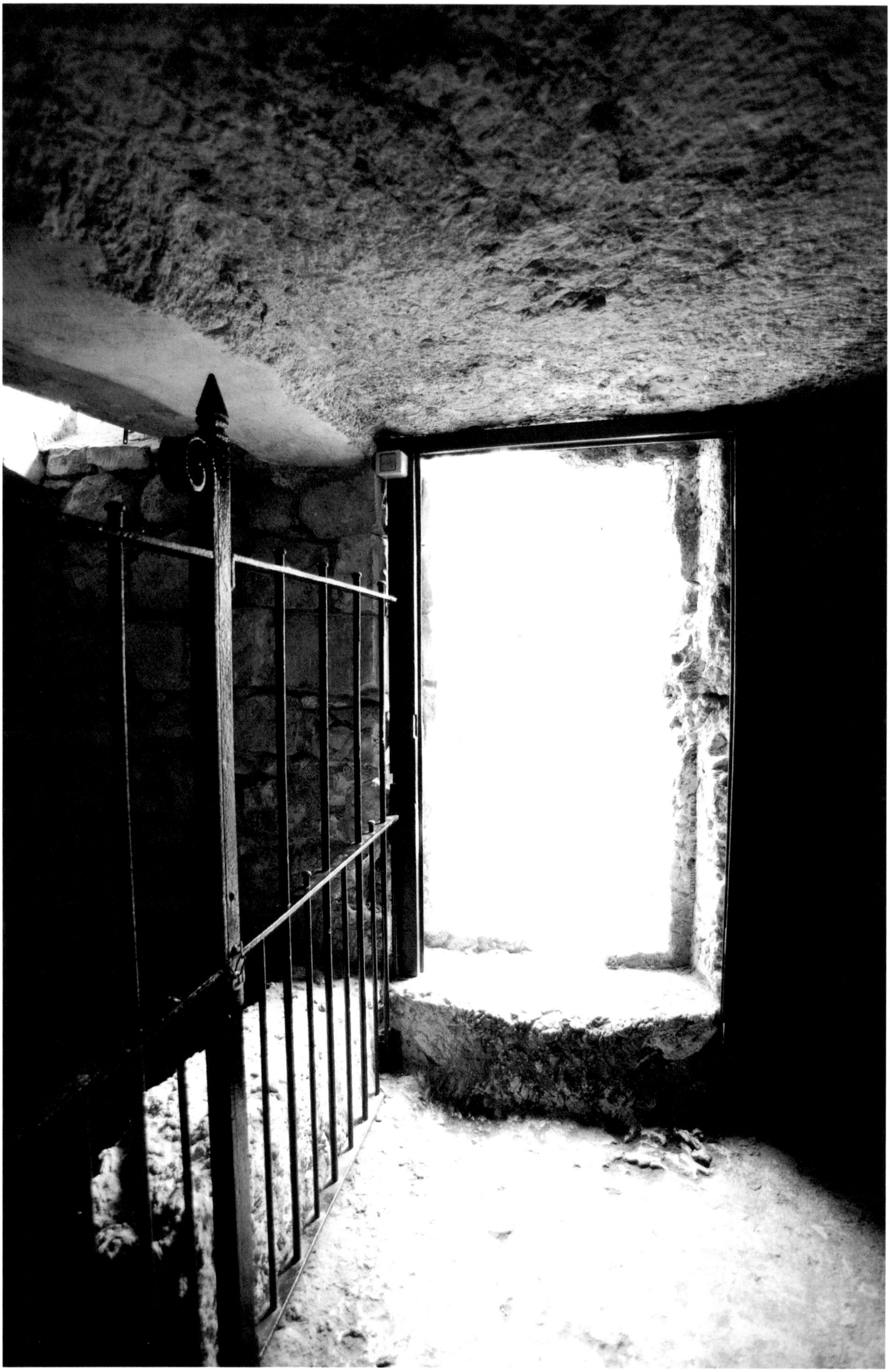

"...Why do you look for the living among the dead?
He is not here; He has risen!"

– Luke 24:5-6 (NIV)

Locations

Determining the location of events that happened two to four thousand years ago is, as you may imagine, difficult. How accurate are the locations in this book?

The church has often damaged its historical credibility by clinging to a nearly absurd level of specificity. There is a church on the Sea of Galilee that is supposedly built over the very rock where Peter and Jesus ate during Peter's restoration. The odds are invisibly tiny that this is the very rock that supported the very Lord of the universe at this pivotal moment in church history. Christians look silly when they make such unsupportable claims. The fixation on which rock is which distracts us from appreciating that the actual restoration probably did take place within several hundred yards of said rock, and certainly within the three miles that make up the Sea of Galilee's western shore.

In another case, the Church of the Holy Sepulcher (the traditional site of Christ's resurrection, venerated by both the Catholic Church and eastern traditions) and the Garden Tomb (an alternate site that could also match the biblical narrative), are about a half mile apart. There are rare cases where historical evidence allows us to be more specific: the synagogue in the town of Capernaum that Jesus almost must have visited and the understandably unchallenged location of the Temple complex in Jerusalem. But for the most part, the search for rocks and relics causes us to cling to assertions that cannot be proved.

If we allow ourselves to dwell on minutia, we can overlook all of the wonderful knowledge that we do have. There are a great number of Biblical sites that we can locate with a high level of accuracy. Oftentimes, archeologists can place these sites within a smaller radius than the distance that may separate you from your nearest grocery store. What is truly important is not the last several yards of resolution that we lack, but rather that we know that these events did not occur in Shangri-la or Oz, but in a real place in our world with a very real person, Lord and Savior named Jesus.

In the early fourth century, the royal consort Helena, mother of the Roman Empire's first Christian emperor, Constantine, embarked on a mission to preserve the holy sites of Palestine. She worked methodically, moving from place to place asking the locals where events had occurred. Given that only 300 years had passed since Christ's earthly life, both physical evidence and oral tradition were readily available. We have respectable knowledge about where the events of the 18th century occurred, and although our record keeping and archeology are more advanced, the Jewish culture that Christianity was rooted in is known for the robustness of its written and spoken history. The churches and monuments built by Helena serve as a starting point for many of the locations in this book.

Not surprisingly, the Bible itself is the best tool for finding these locations. Historians assume that the closer a record is to the event it describes, the more accurate that record is. For events from the New Testament, this puts the Biblical archeologist in remarkably good shape. There is much evidence to put the date of the authorship of the Gospels, which are very location-specific, within the lifetimes of many firsthand witnesses to Christ's ministry. For things of a certain size and permanence (for example, the Temple mount), the Biblical narrative alone can place us within yards of the locations in question.

The Exodus

The events of the Exodus, being furthest from us in time, are some of the most difficult to pin down. For the Israelites' time spent wandering in the desert, the reader must content himself with the broadest definition of "near here" used in the book. Since the whole desert looks the same, I take comfort knowing that if there were pictures from the Israelites' "true route," they likely would be indistinguishable from mine anyway. The location of Mount Sinai/Mount Horeb, the "Mountain of God," is also unknown. The site I visited is the one marked by Helena; the Israelites, avoiding the land of the Philistines along the direct route to the north (Exodus 13:17, 18) might have passed very near it. The monastery at the bottom of the mountain claims to contain both the well where Moses and his wife Zipporah met as well as the original burning bush. My opinion on these claims should be clear, but in the bush's defense, it is over 1700 years old. This is odd for a bush. The Bible does state that the bush is on Mount Sinai, so the monk's claims are at least possible.

Petra is mentioned as a possible site for several important events during the Exodus. Josephus, a first century Jewish historian, identifies the mountain the city is carved into as Mount Hor, the site of Aaron's death. Kadesh-Barnea, where Israel spent the 38 years of their exile, is about ten miles from the mountain. When the time to enter the promised land came, the Israelites from here traveled east to skirt the country of Edom, north through what is now central Jordan, and then finally west to the Jordan river at Jerico.

Tomb of Jesus

The traditional site of Jesus's death and burial is the Church of the Holy Sepulcher on the west side of Jerusalem. There are no pictures of it in this book, because I didn't go there. The site I did visit, known as the Garden Tomb, was not celebrated in antiquity. During the 1800s, several people wrote about a rock outcropping on the north side of Jerusalem that they thought looked like a skull. It does. There was also a tomb buried nearby, and a cistern that could have supported the garden mentioned in the Bible. Archeology tells us that tombs in the first century were typically carved straight back into the rock with the burial chamber placed directly behind the entrance chamber. The burial chamber in the Garden Tomb is located to the right of its entrance chamber, a style more typical of the 5th century B.C. However, the Bible does suggest such a configuration for Jesus's tomb. When the women entered the tomb (in Mark's account), they found the angel sitting to the right, where the body of Jesus had lain. Nonetheless, there is no specific evidence linking the Garden Tomb to the first Easter.

With the exception of the tomb's layout, every argument that supporters of the Garden Tomb use can be applied with equal validity to the Church of the Holy Sepulcher. The traditional site also benefits from an identification 15 centuries earlier than the Garden Tomb. It is also worth saying again that the locations are only separated by ten minutes of brisk walking; so close that if it were somehow proven that the Garden Tomb was the true site, I would not call Helena's seventeen-hundred-year-old research wrong. When weighing all of the evidence, the most likely conclusion is that the resurrection took place in neither of these places, although it almost certainly did take place within sight of either of them. Whether it is the correct location or not, the Biblical account does describe a place very much like the Garden Tomb, and describes a location very close to where the Garden Tomb is.

Of course, the central piece of evidence in the search for Calvary supports both tombs. Both are empty.

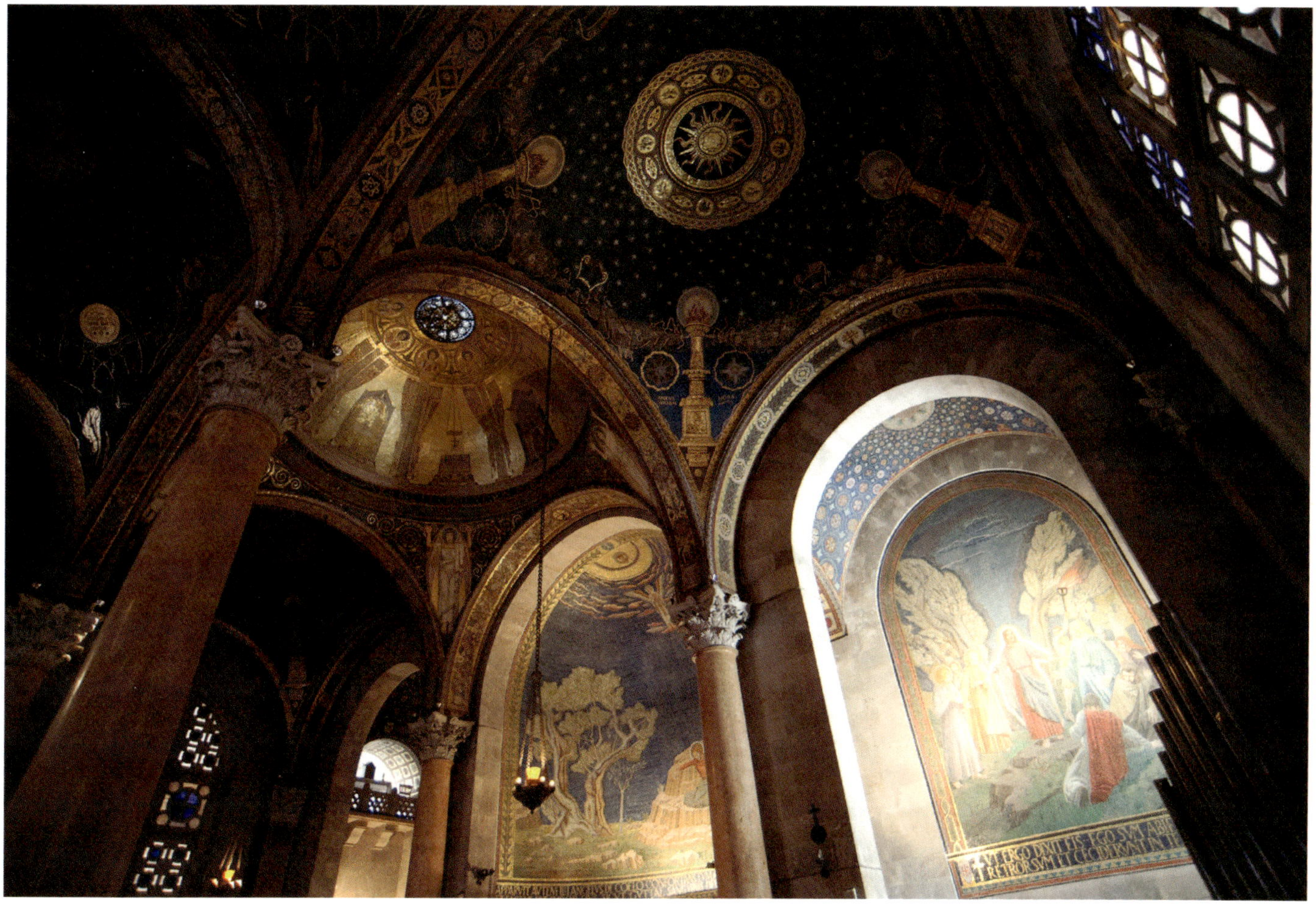

Above: **Church of All Nations in the Garden of Gethsemane**

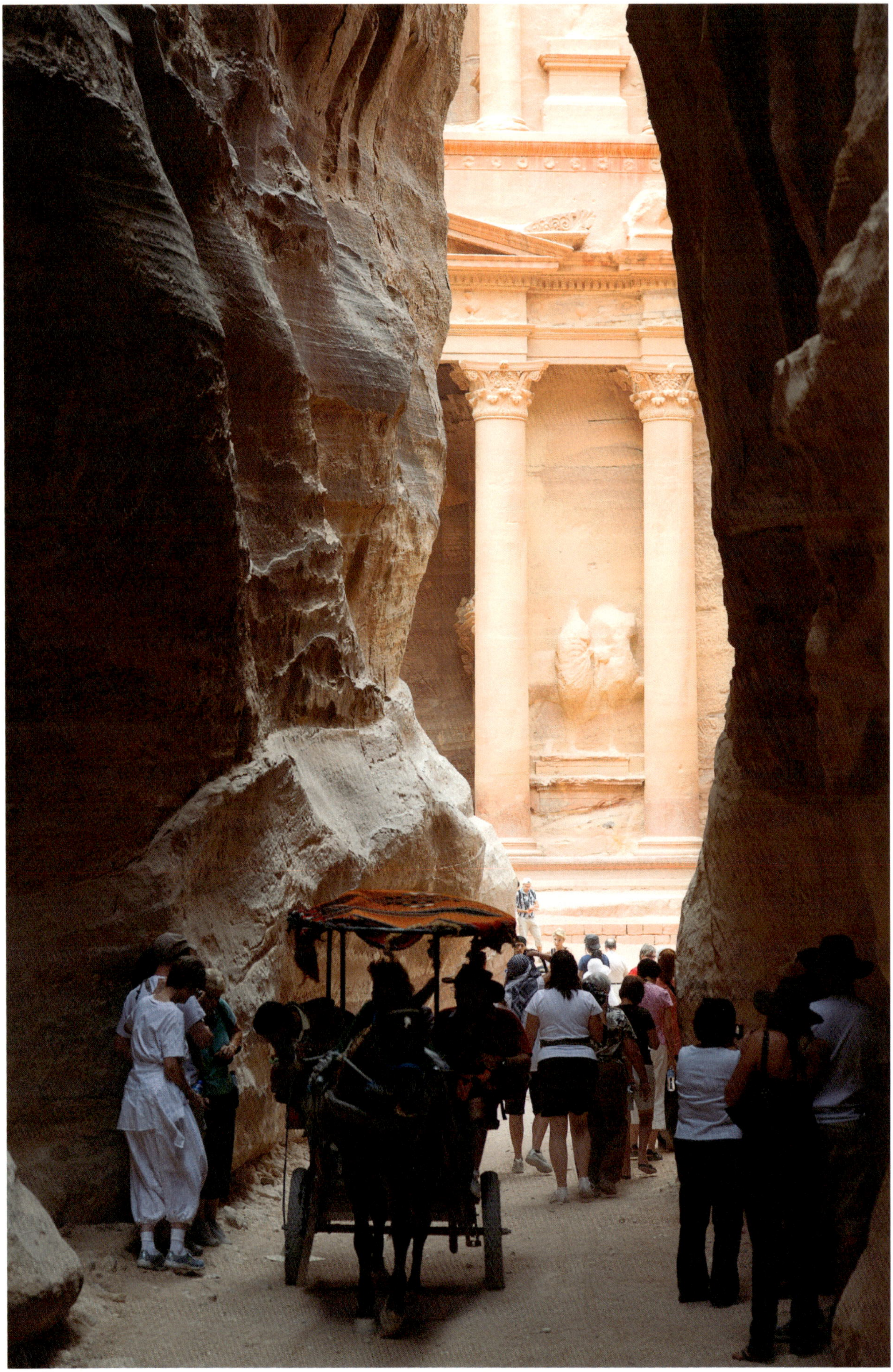

Technical Notes

The photographs in this book were captured as digital images. Editing of the raw data files was limited to global color and brightness adjustments, elimination of geometric distortions, and sensor dust removal. Content within photographs was neither added nor removed. Some photographs are cropped from their original dimensions.

Left: **"The Treasury" at Petra**

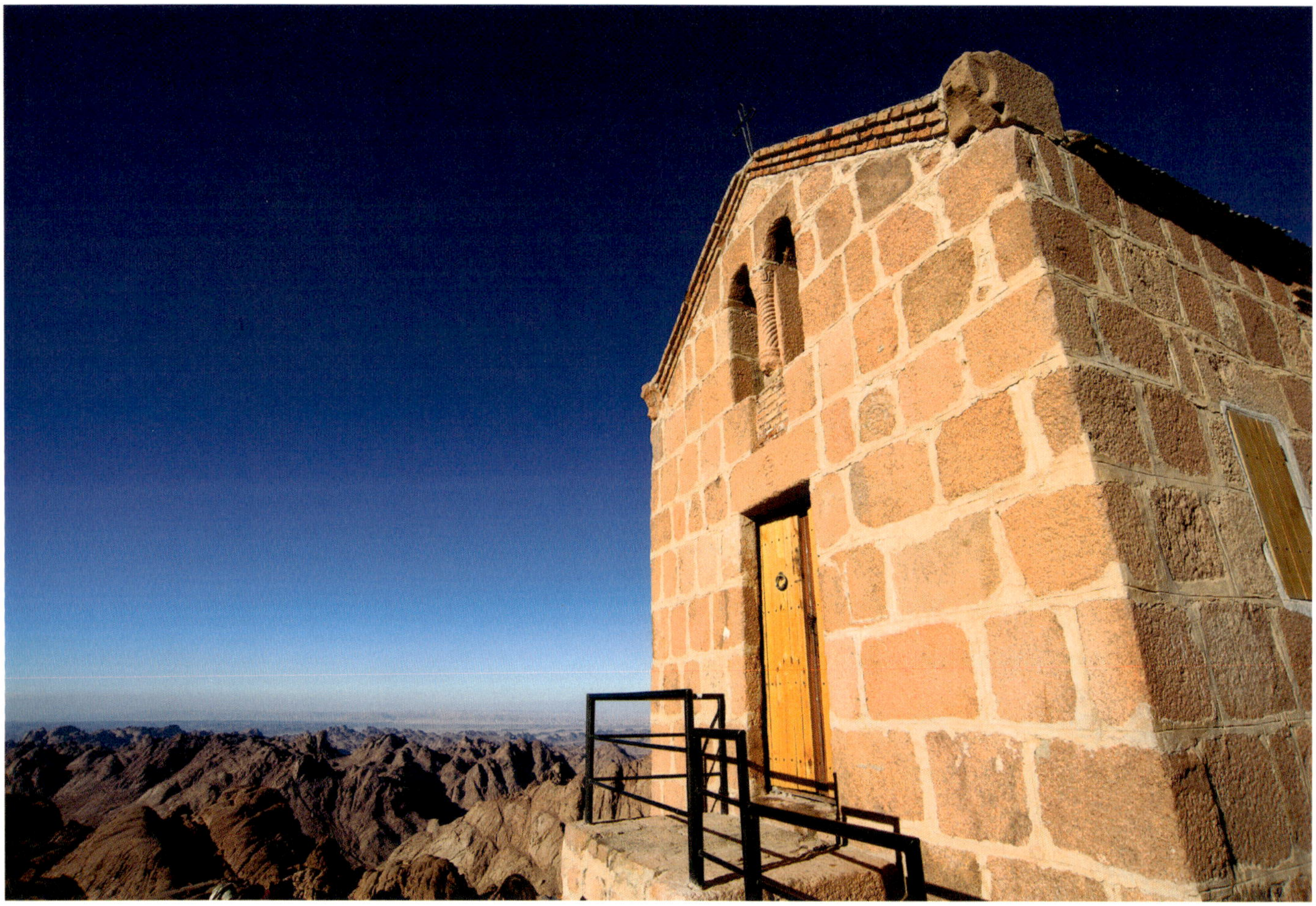

Above: **Chapel at Mount Sinai summit**

Acknowledgments

Many Thanks:

Natalie: For her immense patience and for her encouragement of my photography in general and this project in particular. For great feats of proofreading and for editing to the point of blindness.

Mom and Dad: For letting me take 500 fuzzy pictures of the side of Pike's Peak on real (expensive) film.

Ben and Angie: For enabling my travels in the first place, for their input, and for their enthusiasm for the book.

Olivia: For valuable input on an early draft.

Pastor Lon Solomon of McLean Bible Church: For your knowledge of Israel, which was the starting point for my research.

CPSIA information can be obtained
at www.ICGtesting.com
Printed in the USA
LVIC082247191112
308030LV00004B
* 9 7 8 0 9 8 3 1 4 5 5 1 6 *